# DIANA,
# PRINCESS OF WALES

**DATE DUE**

WOMEN of ACHIEVEMENT

# DIANA, PRINCESS OF WALES

Kristine Brennan

CHELSEA HOUSE PUBLISHERS
PHILADELPHIA

*Frontis:* Princess Diana at a benefit for land-mine victims in Washington, D.C., on June 17, 1997.

**Chelsea House Publishers**
EDITOR IN CHIEF  Stephen Reginald
MANAGING EDITOR  James D. Gallagher
PRODUCTION MANAGER  Pamela Loos
ART DIRECTOR  Sara Davis
PICTURE EDITOR  Judy L. Hasday
SENIOR PRODUCTION EDITOR  Lisa Chippendale

Staff for **Diana, Princess of Wales**
SENIOR EDITOR  Therese De Angelis
ASSOCIATE ART DIRECTOR  Takeshi Takahashi
DESIGNER  Keith Trego
PICTURE RESEARCHER  Sandy Jones
COVER ILLUSTRATION  Michael Deas
COVER DESIGN  Keith Trego

The Chelsea House World Wide Web site address is
http://www.chelseahouse.com

3  5  7  9  8  6  4

**Library of Congress Cataloging-in-Publication Data**

Brennan, Kristine, 1969-
Diana, Princess of Wales / by Kristine Brennan.
144 pp.  cm. — (Women of achievement)
Includes bibliographical references and index.
   Summary: Describes the life and death of the princess who created a sensation by divorcing England's Prince Charles.

ISBN 0-7910-4714-8 (hc). — ISBN 0-7910-4715-6 (pb).

1. Diana, Princess of Wales, 1961-1997—Juvenile literature. 2. Princesses—Great Britain—Biography—Juvenile literature. [1. Diana, Princess of Wales, 1961-1997. 2. Princesses. 3. Women—Biography.] I. Title. II. Series.
DA591.A45D526  1998
941.085'092—dc21                                          98-12929
[B]                                                            CIP
                                                               AC

# CONTENTS

# WOMEN OF ACHIEVEMENT

**Jane Addams**
SOCIAL WORKER

**Madeleine Albright**
STATESWOMAN

**Marian Anderson**
SINGER

**Susan B. Anthony**
WOMAN SUFFRAGIST

**Clara Barton**
AMERICAN RED CROSS FOUNDER

**Margaret Bourke-White**
PHOTOGRAPHER

**Rachel Carson**
BIOLOGIST AND AUTHOR

**Cher**
SINGER AND ACTRESS

**Hillary Rodham Clinton**
FIRST LADY AND ATTORNEY

**Katie Couric**
JOURNALIST

**Diana, Princess of Wales**
HUMANITARIAN

**Emily Dickinson**
POET

**Elizabeth Dole**
POLITICIAN

**Amelia Earhart**
AVIATOR

**Gloria Estefan**
SINGER

**Jodie Foster**
ACTRESS AND DIRECTOR

**Betty Friedan**
FEMINIST

**Althea Gibson**
TENNIS CHAMPION

**Ruth Bader Ginsburg**
SUPREME COURT JUSTICE

**Helen Hayes**
ACTRESS

**Katharine Hepburn**
ACTRESS

**Mahalia Jackson**
GOSPEL SINGER

**Helen Keller**
HUMANITARIAN

**Ann Landers/
Abigail Van Buren**
COLUMNISTS

**Barbara McClintock**
BIOLOGIST

**Margaret Mead**
ANTHROPOLOGIST

**Edna St. Vincent Millay**
POET

**Julia Morgan**
ARCHITECT

**Toni Morrison**
AUTHOR

**Grandma Moses**
PAINTER

**Lucretia Mott**
WOMAN SUFFRAGIST

**Sandra Day O'Connor**
SUPREME COURT JUSTICE

**Rosie O'Donnell**
ENTERTAINER AND COMEDIAN

**Georgia O'Keeffe**
PAINTER

**Eleanor Roosevelt**
DIPLOMAT AND HUMANITARIAN

**Wilma Rudolph**
CHAMPION ATHLETE

**Elizabeth Cady Stanton**
WOMAN SUFFRAGIST

**Harriet Beecher Stowe**
AUTHOR AND ABOLITIONIST

**Barbra Streisand**
ENTERTAINER

**Elizabeth Taylor**
ACTRESS AND ACTIVIST

**Mother Teresa**
HUMANITARIAN AND
RELIGIOUS LEADER

**Barbara Walters**
JOURNALIST

**Edith Wharton**
AUTHOR

**Phyllis Wheatley**
POET

**Oprah Winfrey**
ENTERTAINER

**Babe Didrikson Zaharias**
CHAMPION ATHLETE

*Diana sat on the floor to chat with members of a Bosnian volleyball team who were victims of land-mine explosions, August 9, 1997. The men play by sitting and moving around the court using their arms.*

# 1

# TIME AND SPACE

*"I wanted to give 110% to my work, and I could only give 50."*

—Diana, Princess of Wales, during a BBC-TV
interview broadcast on November 20, 1995

The afternoon of December 3, 1993, found Diana, once the royal family's shining star, feeling like its biggest victim. Her tormentors seemed too numerous to count: her estranged husband, Prince Charles; the entire House of Windsor; the press; and the paparazzi—photographers who relentlessly captured her every move as she struggled to carve out a new identity for herself.

As if these adversaries were not enough to contend with, Diana also wondered just what her new identity would be. This particular afternoon's event—a charity lunch at the London Hilton—would seem ordinary under normal circumstances. But Diana had not lived under normal circumstances for quite some time. Her bitter separation from Prince Charles nearly one year earlier had made her future uncertain. Still legally married to Charles, Diana was technically the future queen of England. She knew that the throne

*Many of Diana's favorite charities involved children. Here she appears at London's Heathrow Airport in 1987 to help send off 300 sick and disabled children on a holiday to Disney World, Florida.*

would never be hers, though. She also realized that a fresh start would be impossible until she resolved her marital woes with Charles.

The possibility of healing the rift with her husband grew more remote each day. Queen Elizabeth II had long been aware of the problems in her son's marriage, but, mindful of Diana's popularity, she initially urged the two to stay together. She knew that without his attractive, youthful wife beside him, Charles stood virtually no chance of winning his people's acceptance as their future king. But by late 1992, even the strong-willed queen acknowledged that Charles and Diana's marriage was severely troubled.

The prince and Buckingham Palace had been dumb-founded by the depth of the public's continued devotion to the princess, even after Charles and Diana's separation was announced in the British Parliament on December 9, 1992. Allegations that Charles was carrying on a long-term affair with another woman, Camilla Parker-Bowles, cemented popular sympathy for Diana. The Palace employed the British press to rebuild the prince's damaged reputation by attacking Diana's. Commentators sneered that Diana was little more than a beautiful mannequin for expensive clothes. They also carped that her volunteer work with AIDS patients, cancer patients, and the homeless was merely a superficial display to enhance her reputation as the "People's Princess"—a woman who understood and addressed the urgent problems facing ordinary people. Some members of the press began to call her the "Princess of Wails" for decidedly un-royal behavior like crying in public and permitting writer Andrew Morton to interview her friends for his book, *Diana: Her True Story*, which painted her as a devoted wife who was mistreated and scorned by Charles.

The assault on Diana's image continued as the royal family attempted to squeeze her out of the spotlight. After the separation was announced, Diana had expressed interest in becoming a roving "goodwill ambassador" for Great Britain. Although Prime Minister John Major enthusiastically supported the idea, the queen refused to let Diana assume such a post. When Diana wanted to establish a Princess Diana Foundation to benefit her favorite charities, Buckingham Palace again refused, fearing that such a fund would divert money and attention from the Prince's Trust, which is mainly dedicated to aiding business and commerce.

Despite the Palace's best efforts, Diana attracted

constant attention, both welcome and unwelcome. Her personal life had been under a microscope since the previous year, when Captain James Hewitt, her sons' former riding instructor, teamed with author Anna Pasternak to write *Princess in Love*, an exposé of Hewitt's affair with Diana. Although admirers excused any adultery on Diana's part by citing Charles's shabby treatment of her, Diana was deeply hurt by Hewitt's betrayal. It was one more painful event that left Diana desperate for some privacy by the end of 1993.

Diana realized, however, that it would be impossible for her, the most photographed woman on earth, to retreat into private life with no questions asked. Furthermore, the princess felt obligated to explain her reasons for withdrawing from the charity work she loved. Immediately after her separation from Charles, Diana had promised the representatives of her favorite charities that her commitment to them would not end. "I want you to be certain of this: our work together will continue unchanged," she had said.

Now, almost a year later, Diana knew that she could no longer keep all of her promises. But she also knew that she could not breach the trust she had built with charitable appeals all over the world. "I thought the only way to do it was to stand up and make a speech and extract myself before I started disappointing and not carrying out my work," she later recalled.

A tangle of emotionally exhausting events had driven her to face the crowd gathered at the London Hilton on December 3. In a brief but dramatic speech, Diana abandoned her usually soft voice and tentative manner to set the record straight.

"I hope you can find it in your hearts to understand and to give me the time and space that has been lacking in recent years," she told her audience. She explained her decision to withdraw, at least temporarily, from public life, including official appearances at state occasions:

*"I adored him," Diana said of Major James Hewitt in a 1995 interview with BBC-TV, confessing her affair with him. But she also declared that "there was a lot of fantasy" in his tell-all book about their relationship. "I was absolutely devastated when [his] book appeared," she recalled.*

When I started my public life 12 years ago, I understood that the media might be interested in what I did. I realized then their attention would inevitably focus on both our private and public lives. But I was not aware of how overwhelming that attention would become; nor the extent to which it would affect both my public duties and my personal life, in a manner that has been hard to bear.

Diana's speech also included a perfunctory thanks to Queen Elizabeth II and Prince Philip for their support throughout her years of public life. But she did not

*The Princess of Wales was showered with gifts at the Institute of Contemporary Art in London on December 16, 1993, where she attended a meeting for an organization that aids the homeless. Two weeks earlier, she had declared her intention to remove herself from the public spotlight; this was her last official appearance for several years.*

mention Prince Charles—an omission that everyone noticed. She told her listeners that raising her two sons would remain her first priority. Princes William and Harry, then 11 and 9 years old, needed "as much love and attention as I am able to give," she said.

Diana's "time and space speech," as it was dubbed, garnered criticism from those who wanted her to slip quietly out of her former life. It even aroused the ire of a good friend, Diana's voice coach Peter Settelen, a former British soap-opera star who had worked with Diana the previous year. Settelen was offended because the princess had not consulted him before making the announcement. She had allowed neither friend nor foe to influence her on this very important occasion.

The Princess of Wales knew that she had reached a personal milestone that day. She had done what was right for her despite stiff opposition. "[I]t did surprise [the royal family] when I took myself out of the game," she said in a 1995 interview. "They hadn't expected that. And I'm a great believer that you should always confuse the enemy."

In 1981, a kindergarten aide named Lady Diana Spencer had become Diana, Princess of Wales, in a fairy-tale wedding that captured the world's imagination. Now, in 1993, the princess was mapping out public-relations strategies against her former husband, the prince—who was now the "enemy." As she hurriedly left the London Hilton that December afternoon, Diana felt more free than she had in nearly 13 years.

But what was she free to do? Her girlhood dream of a stable marriage and family life was destroyed; the strictures of royal protocol offered Diana little hope of recapturing the dream with someone new. Even if she and Charles were to divorce while she was still in her early thirties, remarriage was virtually out of the question. "At this stage it was made clear that any attempt to remarry, or to conduct public relationships with other men, would involve exile abroad—and the loss of her children," wrote royal biographer Anthony Holden in his 1993 book *The Tarnished Crown*. Royal convention permitted the queen to take custody of William and Harry if their mother left Great Britain to live elsewhere.

Diana was not even free to live in a house of her own choosing. After delivering her speech at the Hilton, Diana was understandably anxious to leave London's Kensington Palace. In leaving, Diana wanted only to escape her memories, not to find more space or splendor. After a brief house-hunt, however, she realized that she would need a dwelling that could accommodate security equipment and personnel. But purchasing such an expensive home would contradict her expressed wish to live a more ordinary life—especially at a time when working-class Britons were suffering the effects of an economic recession. "The last thing she wanted," wrote Mary Clarke three years later in *Little Girl Lost*, "was extravagant pictures splashed over the tabloids showing potential new homes when others less fortunate than herself had no choice but to stay where they were."

And so Diana stayed put, in part because she was acutely aware of the feelings of British people from all walks of life. This sensible "common touch" often eluded the born royals. Charles, for example, made a speech that same year disparaging "the technical ease of modern life, the effortlessness and speed of modern communication"—shortly after deplaning from a supersonic Concorde jet.

After her farewell speech, Diana's only hope lay in waiting for Charles and the royal establishment to make more public blunders that showed how out of touch they were with their people. If she could use her innate gift for helping those in need, she knew she could create a new, more meaningful life for herself. But liberation from the British royalty's inner circle carried a high price. Her future as a humanitarian was uncertain. Anthony Holden wrote:

> Diana's public work, as the royals were all too aware, was one of the main sources of her huge popularity. The Queen's advisers remained dubious about her being allowed to continue it as an independent agent. A visibly active Princess of Wales, working outside the royal family, would further undermine Charles's credibility as monarch-in-waiting.

Marginalized by the royal establishment but sought after by the press and paparazzi, the former Lady Diana Spencer would have to fight to continue with her good-works projects. By 1997, when her life was snuffed out in a tragic automobile accident, it was ironically clear that her fight had been successful. Shattered dreams had given way to important work, successful motherhood, and new love. Once derided as the Princess of Wails, Diana had proven to a sometimes fickle but always fascinated public that she would emerge from the shadow of the royal family to become an important figure in her own right.

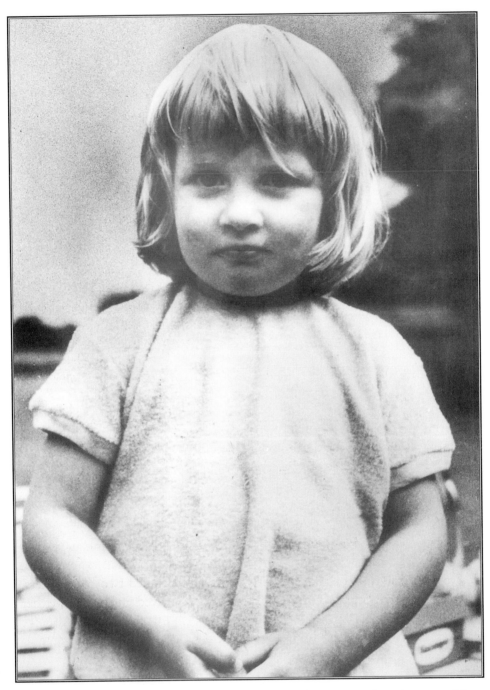

*When Diana (shown here at three years old) was born, her father pronounced her "a perfect physical specimen."*

# 2

# OF CHILDHOOD
# AND CHANGE

*"My father always told me to consider everybody as an equal."*

—Diana, Princess of Wales

The Honorable Diana Frances Spencer weighed in at 7 pounds, 12 ounces when she was born on July 1, 1961. Her father, Edward John "Johnnie" Spencer, Viscount Althorp, pronounced his new daughter "a perfect physical specimen."

On the surface, the story of Diana's birth is simply that of a healthy, much-anticipated baby. But England's entrenched system of hereditary titles had colored her parents' response to her arrival. At the time of Diana's birth her family included two older sisters, Sarah, born in 1955, and Jane, who arrived in 1957. Neither daughter would inherit Johnnie Spencer's title of Viscount Althorp. Only a son could do so, thereby clearing the way for Johnnie to become the eighth Earl Spencer when his own father died.

Eighteen months before Diana's birth, Johnnie and his young wife, the former Frances Ruth Burke Roche, had produced their longed-for son. But the baby, whom the couple named John, was so frail that he died shortly after his birth. In the months after baby John's death, Frances faced a degrading round of physical examinations to determine why she had failed to deliver a healthy male heir. These misguided tests, prompted by meddlesome family members, turned up no physical defects on Frances's part. They did strain the Spencers' marriage, however.

The tragedy preceding Diana's birth led her family to yearn for a healthy boy to replace John. So intense was this wish that they had not bothered to consider a girl's name for their new addition. When their clearly female baby arrived, the Spencers settled on the name Diana Frances—in honor of a family ancestor and Frances herself. Although she was well loved, Diana would grow up haunted by the belief that her birth was a disappointment.

Johnnie and Frances would have to wait three more years for a male heir. Baby Charles joined his three sisters in the nursery of the family home at Park House in 1964.

Diana and her siblings enjoyed a privileged child-hood as members of a landed, aristocratic family. But, as biographer Penny Junor pointed out in *Diana: Princess of Wales* (1983), there were sharp distinctions between their lives and those of the royals, with whom they sometimes mingled. Diana "had a normal child-hood," Junor wrote of Diana, because she "has queued for a bus, run to catch a train, stood at a supermarket checkout, ridden a bicycle through traffic. . . . she has seen how the other half lives in a way that no member of the Royal Family ever could."

Her ability to understand other people's lives would one day make Diana, Princess of Wales, a beloved fig-ure to scores of royal-watchers.

The nursery of Park House and its ever-changing stream of nannies, cooks, and nurses did not cause Diana to suffer any shortage of love and attention. When older sisters Sarah and Jane were not taking class-es with a governess, they were often found in Diana's

nursery, playing with their baby sister's hair or selecting her outfits.

During her infancy, Diana often rode in a carriage as her sisters took afternoon walks around Park House with either Frances or a nanny. Located on the west coast of Norfolk, Park House was part of Sandringham, one of the royal family's country retreats. It was originally built to accommodate extra guests of Sandringham House, which became royal property in 1861 when it was purchased by Edward VII, Prince of Wales.

When Johnnie Spencer installed a heated pool at Park House, little Diana discovered her aptitude for swimming. The pool also attracted the young princes Andrew and Edward, who were frequent guests at the estate. Their brother, Prince Charles, was closer in age to Diana's oldest sister, Sarah. Although some of Diana's relatives report that as a toddler, she once met

*Charles, now the ninth Earl Spencer, with big sister Diana. After their parents divorced in 1969, Diana tried to console her brother, often sitting with him in his room during sleepless nights.*

*Diana as a schoolgirl. Forgoing private tutors, Johnnie Spencer sent Diana and her brother, Charles, to day school in the hope that it would expose them to broader experiences. Years later, Diana herself would follow the same course with her sons, Princes William and Harry.*

the teenaged Prince Charles, neither she nor Charles later remembered it.

Park House also gave Diana and her siblings an expansive playground for their pets. Although she was on horseback by age three, Diana saved her greatest affection for smaller animals. She doted on a series of hamsters, guinea pigs, rabbits, and goldfish during her years at Park House. A cat named Marmalade was a particular favorite of hers, and all of the children loved exploring the grounds with their springer spaniel, Jill.

The Spencer children were not entirely confined to Park House. Frances occasionally took them to see their paternal grandparents at Althorp, an estate that was a museum curator's dream, with dark, eerie rooms filled with works of art. The sour temperament of their grandfather, Jack, the seventh Earl Spencer, probably did little to make Diana feel good about these visits. But Althorp was also home to her beloved grandmother, Countess Cynthia Spencer, who was adored by many for her gentle, helpful manner. In fact, those who still remember Countess Spencer have attributed Diana's warmth and approachability to her grandmother's kindly example.

Not long after Charles's birth in 1964, Diana graduated from her upstairs nursery and joined her sisters in their downstairs "school." Governess Gertrude "Ally" Allen taught the girls the rudiments of math, reading, and history. Favorite after-school activities included expeditions with their mother to the far reaches of Johnnie's farmland to see newborn calves, or to the family's small beach house on the Norfolk coast for picnics.

But Diana's childhood idyll of fresh air and secure routines was soon interrupted by a series of losses. In 1967, Sarah and Jane left Park House for West Heath, a boarding school in Sevenoaks. Accustomed to being taught alongside her beloved older sisters, Diana was painfully aware of their absence.

But the hurt of her sisters' departure was a dull ache compared to the pain Diana felt at the collapse of her parents' marriage. Although the separation came as a shock to Johnnie, to the couple's friends, and—most of all—to their children, Frances viewed it as a long-overdue escape from a stagnant, loveless marriage.

The Honorable Frances Roche, daughter of a baron, had been a starry-eyed 18 when she met 30-year-old Johnnie. He was already the Viscount Althorp and future Earl Spencer, as well as a World War II veteran who had connections to the royal family through his work as equerry (personal attendant) to the queen. He gave up this esteemed position to marry Frances in an opulent wedding that was hailed as the social event of 1954.

Once married, the laconic Johnnie settled comfortably into the role of gentleman farmer. He took his young wife to live with his parents in the stifling atmosphere of Althorp before moving into Park House. Sarah arrived just nine months after their wedding. Frances found Johnnie to be an affectionate father but a dull and distant husband. The birth of each subsequent child, especially the tragically short-lived John, only widened the chasm between them. Frances resented being treated like a young, pretty breeder of pedigrees when Johnnie insisted that they keep trying for a male heir.

After her son Charles's birth, the vivacious Frances fell in love with a married man named Peter Shand Kydd. When the stunned Johnnie agreed to a trial separation in the fall of 1967, Frances moved to an apartment in London. Although she took great pains to explain why she was leaving, the words did little to soothe six-year-old Diana's feelings of abandonment.

That year, Johnnie and Frances shuttled the children back and forth between London and Park House until Christmas, when the family tried to recapture the happiness of past holidays. But instead of feeling joy at her parents' reunion and at the return of Sarah and Jane from school, Diana sadly realized that the family's former life was irretrievably over.

Divorce and child-custody proceedings began soon after. Because of the circumstances of the breakup—and because Frances was up against Viscount Althorp rather than a common man—she lost custody of Sarah, Jane, Diana, and Charles. Frances's own mother, Ruth, Lady Fermoy, supported Johnnie in his proposal to raise the children at Park House. By 1969, the divorce was final.

Although Frances had liberal visitation rights, Diana was affected by her day-to-day absence. Adults around her noticed that she abandoned some of her former

reserve to become more active and outgoing than ever. "Diana," wrote Penny Junor, "never played with any one toy for long. She was on the go all day long, and quite exhausting to be with. This seemed to be her method of dealing with her problems. . . . She chattered constantly from the moment she got up in the morning to the time she went to bed."

No amount of daytime activity could help Diana at bedtime, however. Still a little girl, Diana felt powerless to console her younger brother at night. She often heard him crying for his absent mother but couldn't always summon the courage to tiptoe through the darkened hallways to check on him. "I just couldn't bear it," the grown-up Diana recalled in 1992. "I remember it to this day."

Still reeling from his wife's decision to leave him, Johnnie was initially unsure how to care for two very

*Diana's parents, Johnnie and Frances (center and right), attending a wedding in April 1978, nine years after they divorced. Both parents had remarried by 1976. On the left is Diana's sister Sarah.*

*Diana in 1970, shortly before she left Park House for boarding school at Riddlesworth Hall.*

young children. Sarah and Jane helped out during school breaks, and their two grandmothers—Ruth, Lady Fermoy, and Countess Spencer—stepped in to give Diana and Charles the attention they so desperately needed.

But Frances's absence also meant more time in the care of nannies. "They changed with alarming frequency and ranged from the sweet to the sadistic," Andrew Morton wrote. One of them allegedly disciplined Diana and Charles by banging their heads together. But others were kindly caretakers, like Sally Percival, with whom the Spencer children kept in touch long after her retirement from the nanny business.

As Johnnie emerged from his own sadness, he did his best to compensate for his children's lack of a mother at home. One of his most notable efforts was Diana's seventh birthday party, for which he obtained a camel named Bert from a nearby zoo. Diana and her guests delightedly took turns riding on Bert's back around Park House.

Johnnie later said that he had arranged this grand surprise for his daughter to reward her efforts at school. Diana had started attending school after her parents decided that she and her brother would be busier and happier at a suitable day school than with a private tutor at home. They hoped that interacting with other children would help Diana and Charles escape some of the gloom that had recently descended upon Park House.

Diana and Charles began their formal academic careers at the Silfield School, a small private school in nearby King's Lynn. Charles attended half days in the nursery school class; his sister joined an all-day group for five- and six-year-olds. At school, Diana's nurturing tendencies became pronounced. "She used to enjoy going into the nursery school class and helping the little ones at Silfield, and she was always like a mother hen with Charles," reported Penny Junor.

But their arrival at Silfield also fostered a rivalry between Diana and her studious younger brother. Although Silfield's headmistress, Jean Lowe, remembers that Diana entered school with good reading and handwriting skills, she recalled that the child exhibited no special academic talent. Charles, on the other hand, was recognized as a bright pupil even at age four. "I longed to be as good as him in the schoolroom," Diana later said wistfully.

Nonetheless, Diana's cheerful, helpful demeanor

enabled her to adapt to the classroom. Attending day school was not easy for her at first. She was unaccustomed to mingling with—and sometimes competing with—a whole group of energetic children. But Silfield encouraged cooperation over competition in every aspect, from outdoor sports to academic studies.

With Johnnie's help, the two youngest Spencers successfully made the transition from the protected environment of Park House to a broader world bustling with new friends and experiences. His aristocratic offspring even commuted to and from Silfield School in a car pool that Johnnie himself helped orchestrate. He also arranged for Diana and Charles to visit their mother in London on weekends. In addition to the joy of seeing Frances, Diana now got to take a weekly train ride, which she eagerly anticipated.

Despite the turmoil of her early years, Diana was remembered by Headmistress Lowe, her friends, and the staff at Park House as a child who caused little trouble. In fact, Diana's desire to help and her willingness to try had already become hallmarks of her personality. Penny Junor described Diana as "a great trier" even at an early age. She would later harness this fortitude as she grew into the role of Princess of Wales.

Perhaps Diana's strengths were beginning to emerge because her life was settling into a somewhat predictable pattern as the 1960s came to a close. Her mother married Peter Shand Kydd in 1969. When Diana visited her mother and new stepfather, she soon discovered that Shand Kydd, a wallpaper tycoon, was a fun companion who liked her.

The Kydds had settled on the Isle of Seil, off the coast of Australia, where Frances happily took up breeding and showing ponies. She and Johnnie made joint decisions about their children's education. By the fall of 1970, Diana's parents had decided that she was ready to attend a boarding school, Riddlesworth Hall, two hours away by car from Park House.

Diana resisted the very idea of Riddlesworth at first. "Diana was nine and felt the wrench from her father keenly," Andrew Morton wrote in *Diana: Her True Story—In Her Own Words* (1997). "His decision to send her away from her home and brother into an alien world was interpreted as rejection."

That fall, however, Diana was dressed in Riddlesworth Hall's requisite red blazer and gray pleated skirt. Her trunk was packed; she was also allowed to take one stuffed animal (a green hippo) and one real one (a guinea pig named Peanuts).

Although her father characterized the day he dropped her off as "dreadful," he also realized there was no turning back. His farming interests and community responsibilities kept him away from home for long stretches during the day. At Riddlesworth, Johnnie knew that Diana would be supervised constantly.

But nine-year-old Diana was skeptical. Day school was one thing, but now she was being asked to live away from the only world she had ever known, with more than 100 other girls. It was one more in a series of upheavals.

The first decade of the Honorable Diana Frances Spencer's life was rigorously testing her adaptability. In that sense, her early years would set the tone for things to come.

*Lady Diana Spencer as a young teen.*

# 3

# FINDING HER WAY

*"I'll always remember her as a loving girl."*

—Betty Andrews, former housekeeper at Althorp

Riddlesworth Hall proved to be a happy home for Diana and Peanuts, the guinea pig. The former lived in a dormitory; the latter took up residence in Pets' Corner, a common area filled with small creatures in cages and hutches. Students were given two half-hour breaks a day to feed, play with, and care for their animals. Headmistress Elizabeth Ridsdale devised Pets' Corner as a way to alleviate homesickness among the girls while encouraging responsibility.

The lesson was not lost on Diana, who kept her guinea pig's cage spotless. She became "quite bossy about the way everyone else looked after their animals, and thoroughly disapproved of anyone who tried to shirk her responsibilities," according to one biographer. Her loving care paid off: Peanuts won the Palmer Cup for pets in a Riddlesworth contest.

Diana's victory was in keeping with Riddlesworth's mission state-

*"I adored animals," Diana said of her childhood and adolescence. In addition to her beloved guinea pig, Peanuts, she also had pet hamsters, rabbits, a cat named Marmalade, and "anything in a small cage," as her mother once remarked. Here, 14-year-old Diana is shown on holiday in Scotland with her Shetland pony, Soufflé.*

ment, which promised, among other things, that "every child will have the opportunity to be good at something." Not surprisingly, Diana's other great honor at Riddlesworth was an award called the Legatt Cup for helpfulness. Her academic performance still did not indicate any stirrings of future greatness, but a sense of responsibility and a willingness to help were already pronounced strengths in Diana's budding character.

But Diana was not always demure and well behaved. Buoyed by the presence of a few friends from Silfield School and her cousin, Diana Wake-Walker, Diana Spencer had relatively little difficulty adjusting to sharing a dormitory room with about 10 other girls. She was reserved in the classroom, but friends remember an energetic girl who was capable of egging on other people to feats of mischief. However, Diana completed her four years at Riddlesworth without undue difficulty.

Her teenage years unfolded with the same mixture of reserve and high spirits that had marked her early child-

hood. Diana followed her sisters to West Heath boarding school in the fall of 1973. By this time, the regi-
mented routine of education away from home had
become second nature to Diana.

Schoolwork, however, would never come easily to
her. Diana had difficult acts to follow in Sarah and Jane.
Sarah never completed her education at West Heath,
but it was not for lack of intelligence or ambition. In
fact, she had competed in lacrosse and shone in school
plays while completing six of the O-level (Ordinary)
exams required to complete a General Certificate of
Education (the British equivalent of a terminal high
school diploma; A-level—or Advanced—exams are
required for students wishing to go on to college). It
was Sarah's obstreperous behavior that prompted West
Heath's principal, Ruth Rudge, to send her packing.

Jane, who was in the sixth form (equivalent to the
senior year in high school) when Diana arrived, pre-
sented quite another challenge to Diana. Smart and
conscientious, Jane collected several A-level examina-
tion passes and became a prefect (monitor) during her
career at West Heath.

Although Jane was the worthier role model, Diana
chose to emulate Sarah. She bucked what remained of
her reserved nature and attempted to imitate Sarah's
antics before settling into West Heath on her own terms.

It took a run-in with Miss Rudge to get Diana back
onto the straight and narrow path. She sneaked out of
her dormitory one night on a dare, only to be caught by
the principal upon her return. Both her parents were
contacted about the matter. Despite Miss Rudge's obvious displeasure, Johnnie and Frances were mildly amused
by the idea of their youngest daughter overcoming her
fear of authority—and of the dark—to go AWOL.

Her behavior mellowed somewhat after her noctur-
nal escape, but Diana was still a vigorous young woman
with a strong appetite. She loved food and frequently
tucked into large portions of anything from cereal to

kippers (smoked fish). At 5'10½" tall, she exuded strength and health that would one day contrast sharply with the painfully thin figure she would later cut while in the throes of bulimia.

Diana was also an impressive athlete. Her swimming and diving garnered several awards at West Heath. Although very tall, she could dive gracefully into a pool with minimal splash—prompting her friends to christen this feat the "Spencer special." But even this could not liberate her from the shadow of her two active sisters and a mother who had been "captain of everything" in her day.

Dance was one endeavor that nobody in her family had fully mastered before her, and Diana pursued it with gusto. She was an avid ballet fan who signed up to see *Swan Lake* whenever West Heath offered a field trip to the theater. Diana applied her work ethic to the ballet barre much more assiduously than she ever did to her schoolbooks. This dedication, combined with natural talent, earned Diana first place in a school dance contest in 1976. But the very height that would later make her the envy of so many style-conscious women limited her: she was too tall to pursue a serious career in dance.

Volunteer work posed no such physical restrictions, however. Diana started visiting the elderly, the sick, and the physically challenged while at West Heath because the school encouraged students to serve the surrounding community of Sevenoaks. She soon discovered that she had an innate ability to establish a warm rapport with people of different types and levels of functioning. "Many new school volunteers were apprehensive about visiting. . . . [their] anxieties [were] fed by their fear of the unknown," writes Andrew Morton. "However, Diana discovered that she had a natural aptitude for this work."

Her success stemmed in part from her likability. She was a popular student at West Heath, and some of the friendships she forged were lasting ones. Carolyn Bartholomew, who as Carolyn Pride shared a dormitory room with Diana at West Heath, later lived with her in London. Her friends at West Heath thought enough of her to pool their money and buy her a necklace decorated with the initial *D* for one of her birthdays.

Diana was developing personal charm and magnetism, but her academic growth was another matter. She left West Heath in the late fall of 1977 without even a single O-level pass to her credit. She had essentially failed out of high school—despite staying on for an extra term to try her exams one last time. Friends later attributed this astonishing degree of underachievement to a variety of causes ranging from her phobia of tests to her voracious reading of romance novels by Barbara Cartland.

Whatever the cause, Diana was a rudderless ship when she returned to her father's house. "Home" was no longer cozy, inviting Park House, since Johnnie had inherited the dark, forbidding Althorp estate after his father's death in 1975. When the churlish seventh Earl Spencer followed the sweet-tempered Countess Cynthia Spencer in death (she had died of a brain tumor in 1972), Diana, Jane, and Sarah each got the appellation of "Lady" affixed to their names. Their brother, Charles, stepped into Johnnie's title of Viscount Althorp; Johnnie in turn became the eighth Earl Spencer. His new title necessitated moving his family into the Althorp house.

Diana had always dreaded visits to that eerie place during her grandfather's lifetime, and the prospect of living there was unthinkably horrible. Her family remembers Diana running from room to room as Park House was being emptied, saying goodbye to every nook and cranny of her childhood home.

It was perhaps fortunate that when the family had to leave Park House for Althorp, Diana was still away at school much of the time. Althorp was located in

Northamptonshire, inland from Park House. The vast earldom included about 100 cottages scattered over 13,000 acres of land. Running the estate's affairs therefore consumed most of Johnnie's time. He was sensitive to the disruption the move had caused in Diana and Charles's lives, though, and installed a swimming pool on the grounds to help them feel at home during summer holidays from school.

Sarah and Jane were less affected by the move, because they had long since moved to London and become part of that city's social scene. Diana visited them often but also made the best of the time she spent at Althorp. Its halls may have been stiflingly formal, but they afforded her enough space and privacy to practice her dancing. This extra effort during summers and holidays probably helped her win the West Heath dancing competition in 1976.

Diana's ability to capitalize on her natural gifts buoyed her self-esteem as she floundered in the classroom. Although her extra term at West Heath had not yielded any exam passes, Diana had been made a prefect just like her steady, dependable sister Jane had before her. She also came home bearing the Miss Clark Lawrence Award for service to the school. If ever she doubted her own strengths, those around her noticed Diana's desire to help wherever she was needed as well as her unflagging willingness to try.

Not only did Diana have to adjust to spending more time at Althorp upon leaving West Heath in 1977, but she also had to cope with a new stepmother. On July 19, 1976, Johnnie had quietly married the flamboyant Raine, former Countess of Dartmouth. Like Diana and her siblings, Raine was an aristocrat, first as Lady Lewisham and then as Countess of Dartmouth when her first husband was made an earl. Raine's 28-year marriage to Earl Dartmouth produced four children. She left her former title and family behind for Johnnie Spencer, who was equally smitten with her.

Diana and the other Spencer children were not enamored of Raine, however. Although Raine was the daughter of Diana's literary idol, Barbara Cartland, Diana still disliked the assertive, bouffant-haired stepmother who dominated her father with a carefully manicured—but iron—hand.

By all accounts, Raine Spencer blew into Althorp with the subtlety of a hurricane. She had long been active in local politics, and one of her more notable campaigns was against showing the film adaptation of James Joyce's *Ulysses*—although she herself had never seen it. Raine stormed into Althorp and clamped down on the earldom's expenses. She pared down the house staff, sold off pieces of the deceased seventh earl's art collection, and converted all but the west wing of Althorp into a tourist attraction for paying customers. She also turned away many of the pets that Diana and Charles had brought with them from Park House.

Johnnie gratefully acquiesced to Raine's tightfisted business acumen, and others have acknowledged that were it

*Johnnie Spencer and his second wife, the former Countess of Dartmouth, in the gift shop at Althorp, 1981. Raine, whom Diana and her brother called "Acid Raine," converted most of the earl's home into a tourist attraction shortly after she married him in 1976.*

not for her, Althorp would have crumbled under the weight of its own operating expenses. But none of this endeared her to Diana, Jane, Sarah, or Charles. In her biography of Diana, Penny Junor wrote: "Becoming a stepmother is an unenviable role for any woman, but Raine could have handled the children with more tact. She was, after all, walking into a family whose children had had no mother living with them for eight years and were used to being the center of their father's attention." Junor also rightly points out that the Spencer

*Diana first met her future husband, Prince Charles, while he was dating her sister Sarah (right) in 1977. "I kept out of the way," Diana recalled years later. "I remember being a . . . podgy, no make-up, unsmart lady but I made a lot of noise and he liked that."*

children were old enough not to need Raine's domineering brand of involvement. Sarah and Jane stayed away; Diana had to visit them in London or await their rare weekend trips to Althorp to see them. Although Andrew Morton quotes Raine as saying, "Diana was sweet, always did her own thing," it is likely that Diana simply avoided confronting her stepmother and kept to herself while at Althorp.

Perhaps in an attempt to escape Althorp, Diana took one more crack at school after leaving West Heath. This time she enrolled in Institut Alpin Videmanette, a pricey Swiss finishing school. This facility was supposed to help Diana perfect her French and practice such domestic arts as cooking and sewing. It might well have done those things had Diana devoted less time to honing her skiing technique while there. When Diana flatly informed her parents that they were wasting their money on finishing school, she came home to England for good.

Coming home meant returning to life in the shadow of the rest of her family, though. Her outspoken sister Sarah had always been Diana's heroine. Before Diana departed for Institut Alpin Videmanette, Sarah Spencer's name was being bandied about as the possible future queen of England. Charles, Prince of Wales, had taken a fancy to sharp-tongued, witty Sarah, but their relationship lasted slightly less than one year.

While the romance was still in bloom, however, Sarah sought treatment for anorexia nervosa, and Prince Charles reportedly offered her moral support during her recuperation in a private hospital. By November 1977, when Diana met Prince Charles, Sarah's health was restored. She invited Diana to join them for a day of shooting at Althorp. This early encounter between Prince Charles and Lady Diana Spencer was one that both would remember.

The prince described the younger sister he had met that day as "a very jolly and amusing and attractive 16-year-old—full of fun." But Diana attached little significance to the meeting. Not long after their afternoon together at Althorp, Diana trekked off to finishing school.

Charles, on the other hand, did not forget Diana so easily. After his romance with Sarah fizzled, Charles and Sarah remained friendly. It was therefore not surprising that the prince invited her to his 30th birthday party in November 1978. The real surprise was another name on the Buckingham Palace guest list: Diana's.

After years of life as the youngest sister and the undistinguished student, Lady Diana Spencer was about to mingle with royalty. At 17, the force of her emerging personality was propelling her into the limelight.

*Lady Diana with two of her charges at Young England Kindergarten, where she worked three days a week. By this time she was rumored to be romantically linked with Prince Charles, and photographers had begun pursuing her almost constantly. This photo was one of several that Diana agreed to pose for in the hope of appeasing the ever-present press.*

# 4

# "I SHALL NO LONGER BE ME"

*"What a sad man."*

—Princess Diana on her first impression of Prince Charles

Diana accepted Prince Charles's invitation to his 30th birthday gala. Although he escorted another woman to the party, Charles began to see Diana more often in the following months. Diana later said that Sarah was the first to pick up on the prince's interest in her: "Saw him off and on with Sarah and Sarah got frightfully excited about the whole thing. . . . she saw something happening which I hadn't twigged on to."

At first, Charles invited Diana to outings and dinner parties with his circle of friends. They were generally much older than Diana— and, in her opinion, overly solicitous of the prince. But Charles was still romantically linked with other women at this stage of his friendship with Diana. He never seemed content to stop searching for the ideal mate. In her book *Diana in Private*, Lady Colin Campbell quotes an unnamed member of the prince's staff who characterizes him as a "ditherer" rather than a "doer."

His tendency to dither in the quest for a suitable wife had already cost him dearly. During his twenties, Charles met confident, outdoorsy Camilla Shand. While she had marriage on her mind, Charles feared limiting his options. Only after Camilla had married his friend, military officer Andrew Parker-Bowles, did Charles realize how deeply he loved her.

Charles and Camilla remained close after her marriage, even addressing one another by the maudlin pet names Fred and Gladys. Their friendship, however, could not help Charles obtain what he needed most: a wife. As he reached his thirties, Charles had the unhappy distinction of being the oldest unwed Prince of Wales in the history of Great Britain. He felt pressure from both his anxious parents and his interested subjects to marry and produce an heir to the throne. During an interview when he was 27, he had unwittingly intensified this pressure by pronouncing 30 to be "about the right age to marry."

The Prince of Wales could not run off with just anyone, though. "No royal choice of spouse had been more difficult than Charles's," wrote Anthony Holden. "As heir to the throne, and prospective head of the church . . . [h]e had to get it right." His mother, Queen Elizabeth II, believed that only another person born into royalty would be able to understand the need, in Holden's words, to "put duty before pleasure, submerging her own personality into his."

Royal protocol also forbade Charles to marry a Catholic or a divorcée. As the wife-to-be of the future head of the Church of England, a bride fitting either of those descriptions was taboo. In addition, an unspoken expectation was that the prince's bride be a virgin. But, as Holden wryly points out, virtually no woman alive could meet all of the necessary criteria: "Given the collapse of so many European monarchies in this century, eligible non-Catholic virgin princesses were in somewhat short supply."

But Lady Diana Spencer fit the bill remarkably well. Although not a royal, she was an aristocrat. More important, she was at ease in the royal family's presence because she had known them since her childhood at Park House. Diana also was an especially suitable match because she had had no serious boyfriends prior to meeting Charles. The fact that she was a healthy young woman who dreamed of having children further prompted Charles to move—decisively, at last—in her direction.

Diana's qualifications were lost on some observers, who couldn't understand why the prince would fall for a finishing-school dropout nearly 13 years his junior. Some of the commentary on Diana was harsh: "If she hadn't inherited class or wealth, with her lack of qualifications she would be lucky to get a job selling ice cream in a cinema," groused one biographer in 1982.

Diana's detractors had failed to consider her strong will, however. By the time she was 19, Diana's diffident exterior belied her determination to marry Charles. An anonymous source who attended school with Diana described her as having "the will-power of ten devils." Her critics had also overlooked Diana's instinctive gift for connecting with people.

To her, the Prince of Wales was just another person—and a lonely one at that. As their friendship deepened, Diana proved to be a tender, interested companion. The turning point in their relationship occurred in July 1980, when Diana was invited to a barbecue at the home of Commander Robert de Pass, a mutual family

*Lady Diana outside her flat at 60 Coleherne Court in November 1980. Three months later, Queen Elizabeth announced Prince Charles and Diana's engagement.*

friend. She was seated next to Charles. After making small talk, the two touched on a painful subject for Charles—the 1979 murder of his great-uncle Lord Mountbatten, who was assassinated by members of the Irish Republican Army (IRA).

"You looked so sad when you walked up the aisle at Lord Mountbatten's funeral," Diana told him. "It was the most tragic thing I've ever seen. My heart bled for you when I watched. I thought: 'It's wrong, you're lonely, you should be with somebody to look after you.'"

Diana wanted to be that somebody. Her natural empathy and desire to help touched the prince deeply. He was experiencing firsthand Diana's innate ability to put others at ease. The seemingly shy teenager had reached out to the Prince of Wales as they sat together on a bale of hay. In his eyes, she was suddenly transformed from a "very jolly and amusing" young girl into a potential partner.

Perhaps Diana felt special empathy for Charles's loss because she had very nearly lost her beloved father shortly before Lord Mountbatten's murder. In late 1978, Earl Spencer suffered a stroke—just one day after Diana had predicted to friends that something terrible would happen to him. The comatose earl lingered between life and death for months. Diana's stepmother, Raine, guarded Johnnie's bedside ferociously; she even attempted to forbid Diana and her sisters and brother from seeing their father. Although Diana seethed with resentment against her stepmother throughout her father's illness, she later realized that the woman she and her siblings privately dubbed "Acid Raine" had virtually willed Earl Spencer back to life. Johnnie was on the road to recovery by early 1979.

The near-death of her father was a dark cloud over an otherwise happy time in Diana's life. Although the young woman enjoyed increasing attention from Prince Charles after that 1980 barbecue, she behaved like any other teenager ready to strike out on her own. After leaving West Heath and the Swiss finishing school, Diana was anxious to follow her sister Sarah to London. She was a frequent visitor to Sarah's apartment there, although Andrew Morton notes that she no longer imitated Sarah's wilder ways: "She didn't smoke and never drank. . . . Noisy nightclubs, wild parties or smoky pubs were never her scene."

Diana's sedate lifestyle notwithstanding, her parents forbade her to have her own flat (apartment) until she turned 18. Diana bemoaned their decision in typical adolescent fashion. Her 18th birthday present more than made up for the disappointment, though. In July 1979, Diana moved into a three-bedroom flat at 60 Coleherne Court in London—purchased for her by Johnnie and Frances. She was anxious to share her good fortune with friends, so Lady Diana Spencer became landlady to Carolyn Pride (now Bartholomew), an old friend from school. After two other friends briefly passed through, Anne Bolton and Virginia Pitman came to stay.

"Diana later looked back on those days at Coleherne Court as the happiest time of her life," wrote Andrew Morton. "It was juvenile, innocent, uncomplicated and above all fun." Diana made light of her role as landlady: she was "Chief Chick" of the house, according to a label on her bedroom door. Her idea of fun could be as sophomoric as sneaking out at night with Carolyn to pelt a friend's car with eggs. Gin distillery heir James Gilbey's Alfa Romeo became one of Diana's targets after he canceled a date with her.

Perhaps it was her own childlike high spirits that drew Diana to the idea of working with children. She first tried to combine her love for children with her talent in dance. After applying in early 1979 for a job with Betty Vacani, a famous dance teacher who had instructed many of the young royals, Diana was soon assisting with children's dance classes at Vacani's London studio. She was out of a job by spring, however, having torn

*Charles and Diana in casual dress on a visit to Balmoral, the queen's Scottish estate, two months before they were married. The first signs that Diana was suffering from bulimia appeared during the five months between her engagement to Charles and their wedding in July 1981.*

tendons in her left ankle that March while skiing in the French Alps. Diana's injury took months to heal, rendering her useless in the dance studio.

Her short stint at Betty Vacani's school of dance was not her first experience working with children, however. Her sisters often referred her to their friends who had children, supplying her with numerous jobs as a nanny. Diana also took on childcare work through an employment agency called Knightsbridge Nannies. Of all of her numerous odd jobs and pursuits—housecleaning for her sister Sarah, waiting tables at private banquets, taking cooking classes—Diana's work with children interested her the most.

By the time her ankle was completely healed, Diana had found another job that suited that interest perfectly. A kindergarten in Pimlico called Young England offered her a part-time position supervising the pupils' playtime, dancing, and crafts. Her genuine warmth and ability with the children were obvious to her employers. Soon, Diana's hours increased from just a few afternoons each week to entire days spent teaching, playing with, and cleaning up after her diminutive charges. On the days she was not working at Young England, Diana was nanny to an American child named Patrick Robinson. She relished both jobs.

Diana's employment with Young England and the Robinson family coincided with Charles's efforts to woo her. Although she had grown up practically next door to Queen Elizabeth and her children, Diana was unprepared for the rapt attention she received, both from Charles and from the public. Reporters quickly dubbed her "Shy Di" after her habit of hunching her shoulders and averting her eyes from the cameras that began following her wherever she went.

Diana's critics and admirers have since debated the truth of her apparent shyness. Her own step-grand-mother, Barbara Cartland, attributed Diana's stooped posture before the cameras to her discomfort over her height. Diana critic Lady Colin Campbell quoted Cartland as saying that "Shy Di" in fact "had a distinct personality and was not a person, whether she spoke or not, whom one could ignore." However, Mary Clarke, a former nanny of Diana's, claimed in her book *Little Girl Lost* that she was only partially successful in teaching nine-year-old Diana to make eye contact when meeting new people because the child "was genuinely shy, and it always took time for people to discover the real Diana."

Whatever the reason for her apparent bashfulness,

the British public seemed determined to discover "the real Diana" by any means necessary. Photographers began keeping vigil outside 60 Coleherne Court. Inside, Diana fielded constant telephone calls from reporters wanting a direct quote from the prospective queen of England.

Undaunted, Diana enlisted the aid of her friends to engage the press in a continual game of cat and mouse. Carolyn would drive Diana's conspicuously sporty red car from their flat to lure away photographers. Once the coast was clear, Diana herself would walk out of 60 Coleherne Court—often into a waiting car driven by a member of Prince Charles's staff. Even her maternal grandmother, Ruth, Lady Fermoy, got into the act by lending Diana her car to elude the press. On New Year's Day, 1981, Diana drove to Sandringham to join the prince, attracting no attention as she pulled away in her grandmother's conservative silver Volkswagen. She later told of making a rope out of knotted bedsheets and climbing out a window to sneak away for one meeting with Charles.

Work was one place from which Diana could not sneak away. The children at Young England were sometimes upset by the popping flashbulbs that surrounded Diana. One day, hoping to appease photographers once and for all, the reluctant darling of the tabloids agreed to pose for a few moments outside of the school. When she saw the resulting pictures, however, Lady Diana Spencer was mortified to discover that her sheer skirt appeared transparent in the sunshine. Although Prince Charles laughed it off—and complimented her on her shapely legs—Diana was profoundly embarrassed.

Diana was very careful to maintain her polite, cheerful demeanor in public, although she later admitted to Andrew Morton that during this time she "cried like a baby to the four walls" of her flat. Both Charles and the palace press office ignored her pleas for help in handling overzealous reporters.

*This official engagement portrait of the Windsors, taken by Lord Snowdon, shows little of the trepidation Diana felt about her upcoming marriage to the prince.*

*Diana at her first official appearance on March 10, 1981. Unschooled in royal decorum, Diana was criticized for the gown's color and plunging neck-line. "Don't worry," Princess Grace of Monaco said jokingly to Diana later that evening. "It will get a lot worse."*

She was not deterred from pursuing her romance with the prince, however. As 1981 began, Diana anxiously awaited a proposal from Charles. If, as some of her critics later claimed, she was a master manipulator determined to become the Princess of Wales at all costs, Diana had already begun paying dearly in terms of lost privacy.

On the evening of Friday, February 6, Charles

arranged to see Diana at Windsor Castle, 22 miles west of London. He had just returned from a skiing holiday in Klosters, Switzerland, but before his return, he called Diana to say that he wanted to ask her something.

Although Diana had braced herself for his proposal, she caught herself giggling when Charles finally asked her to marry him. Perhaps Diana's girlish laughter was her only defense against a sense of foreboding. Even as Charles reminded her that she would one day be queen of England, her instincts told her otherwise. "You won't be Queen but you'll have a tough role," she recalled thinking then. Diana joyously agreed to marry her prince anyway.

Unable to contain the big news, Diana returned to Coleherne Court that night and told her flatmates. "Everybody screamed and howled and we went for a drive around London with our secret," she told Morton. The only other people privy to the engagement were Diana's parents and siblings. Two days after Charles's proposal, she went with her mother and stepfather to their sheep farm in New South Wales, Australia. Peter Shand Kydd, in particular, enjoyed outrunning the press there. He was also happy to help his stepdaughter enjoy what everyone realized was probably her last chance to vacation in private. The trip included a 10-day stay at a family friend's beach house, where Diana made wedding plans with her mother, caught up on sleep, and indulged in a lot of swimming. She was troubled, however, because Charles did not call her during the three weeks she was away.

Upon her return to Coleherne Court, Diana was greeted by a palace staff member bearing a bouquet. She knew that Charles himself had not selected the flowers for her because no card was attached. Nevertheless, she chose to overlook this second slight and prepared to move out of her beloved apartment. The royal family wanted her to stay in Clarence House, the Queen Mother's home in London. Nineteen-year-old

Diana obeyed unquestioningly.

The queen officially announced the prince's engagement to Diana on February 24, 1981. The night before, Diana sadly bid farewell to her three girlfriends and was escorted by a bodyguard to Clarence House. Even the guard felt compelled to remind her that this was her last night of life as she had known it.

She entered the second-floor apartment that had been prepared for her, but nobody was there to greet her. Staid, silent Clarence House was a stark contrast to Diana's noisy, happy surroundings at 60 Coleherne Court. Her camera-ready veneer of happiness wore thin. In *Diana: Her True Story—In Her Own Words*, Andrew Morton criticized the royal establishment for leaving a naive young kindergarten aide to fend for herself as her life changed drastically. "The popular myth paints a homely picture of the Queen Mother clucking around Diana as she schooled her in the subtle arts of royal protocol," Morton wrote. "In reality, Diana was given less training in her new job than the average supermarket checkout operator."

Perhaps out of trepidation, however, Diana appeared to ignore all indications of trouble. On the day their engagement was announced, a television interviewer asked the couple if they were in love. "Yes. Whatever 'in love' means," was Charles's ominous answer; Diana piped in with, "Of course!"

Her decisions were governed by a girlish sense of wonder: she picked her engagement ring from a splendid assortment because its 18-carat sapphire "was the biggest." Diana's choice of dress for her first royal event—a strapless black evening gown with a plunging bustline—drew criticism from Charles because of its color and overt sexiness. Thinking that black was a stylish color, the 19-year-old felt hurt because her only intention had been to wear "a real grown-up dress" that night.

Swept up in what she would later call a "fairy story,"

Diana suppressed any misgivings and counted the days until her July wedding. She tried to alleviate some of her tension through dance. Teacher Wendy Mitchell regularly visited Buckingham Palace with Lily Snipp, the pianist from West Heath School, to give Diana ballet and tap lessons. In her diary, Snipp later quoted Diana as she counted down the days to her nuptials. "In 12 days time I shall no longer be me," Diana said sadly. Locked away from familiar routines and people, Lady Diana Spencer prepared to give up a part of herself forever.

*Shortly before their wedding, Prince Charles, wearing the full dress uniform of a commander in the Royal Navy, poses for a formal portrait with Princess Diana, dressed in emerald green silk taffeta.*

5

# "KNOCK 'EM DEAD"

*"With Prince Charles by my side, I cannot go wrong."*

—Lady Diana Spencer during her engagement

Not all of Diana's misgivings about her upcoming marriage could be dismissed as mere pre-wedding jitters. About two weeks before the ceremony, she discovered physical evidence that she was not first in Charles's affections. Diana intercepted a package at the Buckingham Palace office she shared with several members of Charles's staff. In one of the earliest demonstrations that she was not just "Shy Di," she overruled the objections of the prince's personal assistant and opened it. What she found stopped her in her tracks: a gold bracelet with a blue enamel charm bearing the initials *F* and *G*. "Fred" apparently wanted to give "Gladys" a token of love, even though his wedding to Diana was just days away.

Diana confronted Charles immediately. He protested that Camilla Parker-Bowles was nothing more than a dear friend—and that he still intended to give her the gift. "So rage, rage, rage!" is how Diana later described her reaction.

Rage notwithstanding, Diana lost the argument. Two days before the wedding, Charles personally delivered the bracelet to Camilla. While eating lunch with her sisters that day, Diana expressed her reservations about marrying Charles. Although they listened sympathetically, Sarah and Jane's final verdict was, "Well, bad luck, Duch [Diana's childhood nickname, short for 'Duchess']." They cajoled her out of canceling the wedding by joking that her likeness was already "on the tea-towels," referring to the many souvenirs being turned out to commemorate the event.

Under intense pressure throughout this period, Diana sometimes failed to keep her inner turmoil hidden from public view. Shortly before the wedding, she burst into tears while watching a polo match and left the grounds. This display of vulnerability set tongues wagging and, of course, threw the press into a frenzy of speculation about Diana's readiness for marriage. As she tried to keep her private troubles to herself, Diana's outward appearance changed. In only five months, her waist shrank from a healthy 29 inches to a sylphlike $23\frac{1}{2}$. Although she was not chubby to begin with, she was determined to lose the rounded contours of adolescence and cut a sleek figure at her wedding. But Diana maintained her new slimness because she suffered from bulimia, an eating disorder that would cast its shadow over her life for more than a decade.

Victims of bulimia binge, or eat an excessive amount of food in one sitting. Then, fearing obesity and the lack of control that heaviness symbolizes to them, bulimics purge their bodies of food by making themselves vomit or by overusing laxatives. Psychologists believe that one of bulimia's major causes is the victim's fear that she (most bulimics are women) is inadequate and unworthy of love.

Diana later explained her struggle with bulimia by saying, "You inflict it upon yourself because your self-esteem is at a low ebb, and you don't think you're

worthy or valuable." It is not surprising, then, that Diana began bingeing and purging regularly during her stay at Clarence House. She ate ravenously without gaining weight.

The world outside of Clarence House crackled with the energy of a country's dreams as the wedding drew near. In the summer of 1981, Great Britain buckled under the weight of a severe economic recession. The marriage of Prince Charles to a beautiful girl hand-picked from obscurity was a welcome distraction. Although the wedding was scheduled for July 29, royal-watchers began

*The Prince and Princess of Wales rode in a horse-drawn carriage on their way to Buckingham Palace after their wedding ceremony on July 29, 1981. Riding to the wedding reception amid cheering crowds was "wonderful," Diana recalled. "Everybody hurraying, everybody happy because they thought we were happy."*

*Prompted by the jubilant throng outside Buckingham Palace, the royal newlyweds exchanged their first public kiss. Despite her misgivings, Diana said of her wedding day, "I had tremendous hopes in my heart."*

camping out on London's Fleet Street days in advance. Diana and Charles's guest list numbered 2,500; an estimated 15,000 others visited St. Paul's Cathedral as it was being readied for the ceremony.

As Jane kept Diana company on the night of July 28, a celebratory fireworks display dazzled crowds in Hyde Park. Diana herself was dazzled that night by a gesture from Charles that momentarily eased her doubts. He sent her a signet ring identical to the one he wore, along with a card saying, "When you come up, I'll be at the altar for you tomorrow. Just look 'em in the eye and knock 'em dead." For a girl who was once too self-conscious to take speaking roles in school plays, the prospect of taking marriage vows in front of some 750 million television viewers around the world was daunting.

At around 5:00 A.M. on Diana's wedding day, she and Jane awoke to the sounds of revelry outside. Diana breakfasted on coffee, then met with the squadron of professionals who would handle her hair, makeup, and gown. The billowing, romantic gown was the product of a husband-and-wife design team, David and Elizabeth Emmanuel, and three months of hand-sewing by seamstress Nina Missetzis. Missetzis remembers pressing the silken gown and its 25-foot train in Diana's bedroom at Clarence House. The soon-to-be princess had the unnerving experience of watching TV coverage of her own wedding as she waited to get dressed. "She seemed very nervous," the seamstress remembered. "She said, 'Do I really have to go out in front of all these people?'"

But Diana knew that she did. By 10:30, she was riding to St. Paul's Cathedral in a glass coach. She was accompanied by her jubilant father, who, in Diana's words, "waved himself stupid" as they drove past the well-wishers who thronged the streets of London. Although recovered from his near-fatal stroke, the earl still had difficulty walking without assistance. Even so, he was determined to give his youngest daughter away at the altar. Fighting to stay calm as Johnnie leaned on her all the way down St. Paul's 330-foot aisle, Diana focused on getting her father to the altar—and on executing a perfect curtsy to the queen. On the way, Diana glimpsed Camilla Parker-Bowles in the congregation and hoped the older woman would now be safely relegated to Charles's past.

But happy thoughts then washed over her reservations. "I remember being so in love with my husband that I couldn't take my eyes off him," Diana said later. "I just absolutely thought I was the luckiest girl in the world."

The millions of onlookers who found themselves "knocked dead" by Diana's youthful radiance would have agreed. Robert Runcie, then archbishop of Canterbury, officiated. "Here is the stuff of which fairy tales are made," he intoned at the start of the hour-long ceremony. He could not have been more correct. Diana's mind was reeling. "I thought the whole thing [getting married] was hysterical . . . in the sense that it was just . . . so grown up and here was Diana—a kindergarten teacher. The whole thing was ridiculous!" she later confessed to Andrew Morton.

Although she appeared poised, Diana couldn't hide her nervousness entirely. When she made her vows to Charles, Diana addressed him as Philip Charles Arthur George, reversing his first two names. Charles likewise made a small mistake when he promised to share his "goods"—rather than his "worldly goods"—with his bride. Diana recovered from her minor gaffe with a graceful curtsy to her regal mother-in-law after the vows were completed.

In the span of an hour, Diana had entered St. Paul's Cathedral as an insecure kindergarten aide and emerged as Her Royal Highness, the Princess of Wales. An estimated 600,000 spectators cheered and waved to the newest royal couple as their carriage took them back to Buckingham Palace for wedding photos and a champagne brunch.

The festivities at the palace seemed remarkably like those that have surrounded less illustrious newlyweds since time immemorial. Rooms full of gifts and 168 pounds of wedding cake notwithstanding, the couple greeted 120 guests and posed for countless pictures. Diana recalled that throughout this dizzying whirl of activity, her new husband did not touch her, and they spoke very little to one another. She attributed this silence to physical and mental fatigue that left them both feeling "shattered."

Their exhaustion was not apparent, however, when Diana and Charles appeared on the Buckingham Palace balcony to greet the crowd gathered below. "Kiss her!

Kiss her!" people shouted. Although the exchange between the couple was inaudible, witnesses in the crowd believed that they could read Diana's lips saying, "Why ever not?" Charles gave Diana a chaste kiss that delighted the onlookers. Even this small gesture was a bold move for a member of the Windsors, a family characterized by royal self-restraint that bordered on frostiness. It appeared that Diana was already injecting the monarchy with her youthful warmth and vitality.

This was not Diana's first attempt to rewrite the royal rule book, though. As she planned the wedding, Diana had asked the archbishop of Canterbury to omit the bride's vow to "obey" her husband. Her wish had been carried out. She would later learn that effecting change was not always as simple as that.

The newly designated Princess of Wales would soon discover just how much she was expected to learn. Her honeymoon turned out to be a time of rigorous on-the-job training for royal life. But as she and Charles pulled away from Buckingham Palace in their coach—playfully decorated with a "Just Married" sign by Princes Andrew and Edward—Diana's heart brimmed with hope.

*The Princess of Wales accompanying the Queen Mother to the "Trooping of the Colors" ceremony commemorating Queen Elizabeth's birthday. In her 1995 interview with BBC-TV, Diana described her royal status as "isolating," but added that "you couldn't indulge in feeling sorry for yourself; you had to either sink or swim."*

# 6

# DESPERATELY TRYING

*"[Y]ou had to either sink or swim. And you had to learn that very fast."*

—Princess Diana during a 1995 BBC-TV
interview, on her first months as a royal

The Prince of Wales and his new princess awoke to their first full day of married life at Broadlands, the Hampshire home of the late Lord Mountbatten. Charles's parents, Queen Elizabeth II and Prince Philip, had chosen the same site for their own honeymoon 34 years earlier. Charles and Diana stayed there for just two days of much-needed privacy before boarding the royal yacht *Britannia* for a cruise to Gibraltar, a British colony off the southern coast of Spain.

Once the couple was aboard ship, the differences between Diana and Charles became more prominent. The prince's formal ways persisted even after they had set sail on the Mediterranean Sea. The ship's crew—officers of the Royal Navy—dined with the honeymooners every night. Diana found this intrusive, but she soon made a far more disturbing discovery.

*Even before their marriage, Diana had well-placed suspicions about Prince Charles's relationship with Camilla Parker-Bowles. "There were three of us in this marriage, so it was a bit crowded," she would say after her separation from Charles.*

She and Charles were entertaining Egyptian president Anwar al-Sadat and his wife aboard the *Britannia* when Diana noticed the unusual cuff links her new husband wore to dinner. Their design incorporated two intertwined Cs—"Charles" and "Camilla," as Diana immediately surmised. "And boy, did we have a row," she recalled. The cuff links stayed; Diana's insecurity grew. The fact that she was forcing herself to vomit four or five times a day did little to help Diana feel in control of the situation and worsened her health.

Despite her private anguish, 20-year-old Diana appeared cheerful during the state dinner with the Sadats. Her natural warmth and enthusiasm got the better of her when it was time to bid them goodbye. As President and Mrs. Sadat prepared to disembark at Egypt's Port Said, Diana gave both of them farewell kisses. Innocent as this breach of royal protocol was, it drew disapproval from Charles. Rather than offering constructive criticism, however, he demanded that his courtiers train Diana more thoroughly in appropriate royal behavior. "Charles seemed to regard the spontaneous Diana as a kind of rambunctious puppy," one writer remarked in an analysis of the ill-starred marriage.

Diana's natural gregariousness continued to cause her difficulty even after she and Charles left the *Britannia* for dry land. They stayed at Scotland's Balmoral Castle from August to October of 1981. With its misty hills and peaceful woods, Balmoral was paradise for the prince. But though Diana accompanied him to his secluded Highland retreat, she was more comfortable in the trendy shops and restaurants of London. Her idea of fun clashed with Charles's favorite activities.

"Charles used to want to go for long walks around Balmoral the whole time when we were on our honeymoon," she recalled. "His idea of enjoyment would be to sit on top of the highest hill at Balmoral. It is beautiful up there. I completely understand," she recalled, "but I knew there was something in me that hadn't been awoken yet and I didn't think this was going to help!" Although she tried to appreciate her husband's need for quiet contemplation, Diana was upset by his apparent disregard for her desires, and she became even more so when Charles went off fishing and hunting without her during their honeymoon.

According to Diana biographer Lady Colin Campbell, Charles was simply not given to the overt displays of emotion that Diana craved. "He was an individual who had been forced, through circumstance and training, to stand on his own," she wrote:

> Diana was not. She wanted someone to complete her identity, to live out her romantic fantasies with her, to pay constant attention to her, to share every waking hour with her, in never-ending bliss. . . . Diana had chosen a man who was constitutionally incapable of such absorption in another human being.

The couple's age difference also contributed to Diana's unhappiness. Friends of Prince Charles who visited Balmoral were, as a rule, much older than Diana, but as Princess of Wales she was now higher in rank than they were. They treated her "like glass," as she told Andrew Morton—bowing, curtsying, addressing her as "Your Royal Highness" and "ma'am." This disconcerted her greatly. "As far as I was concerned I was Diana," she later said of this confusing time.

Diana was so disoriented by her transformation from shy high-school dropout to Her Royal Highness that her bulimia raged out of control. She grew rail-thin at Balmoral. Although her sister Sarah had overcome another eating disorder, anorexia nervosa, only a few years earlier, Diana was too embarrassed to confide in her. Her other sister, Jane, was not always available because she was now the wife of Sir Robert Fellowes, the queen's press secretary. Diana felt that she could not even turn to her old friends from 60 Coleherne Court: her shame in failing to become the fairy-tale

*Diana on a visit to a London children's hospital in 1982. Although the royal family—and Diana herself—believed that the media's fascination with her would die down after the wedding, it only intensified.*

princess that everyone hoped for was too great.

Despite his inability to understand Diana's emotional distress, the prince did try to ease her transition into royal life. Charles enlisted his mentor, South African philosopher Sir Laurens van der Post, to speak with Diana while she was at Balmoral. When this didn't help, her husband and in-laws sent her to London for psychiatric care. Diana, meanwhile, was convinced that if she were just given time to adjust—or better yet, were patiently instructed in her new role—the royal family could call a halt to the parade of therapists they were summoning. "It was me telling them what I needed," she recalled. "They were telling me 'pills'!" Diana's treatment was not unlike that experienced by her own mother 22 years earlier, when Frances submitted to demeaning medical examinations after the death of her newborn son.

The psychiatrists were silenced, however, when Diana discovered in October that she was pregnant. She was elated by the news; now she would no longer be urged to take the tranquilizers and other anti-anxiety drugs that the doctors were prescribing for her.

Diana needed time to reflect upon the sweeping changes she had undergone, but none was available. The same month she learned of her pregnancy she began taking on official duties, the first being a three-day trip to the principality of Wales. Throughout the visit Diana fought morning sickness as she accompanied Charles on "walkabouts"—appearances where they greeted their subjects on foot. She endeared herself to the Welsh people by dressing in green and red, the national colors of Wales. She did not, however, dress sensibly against the raw, rainy weather that followed them everywhere. "When the rain was pouring down and she refused an umbrella," wrote Lady Colin Campbell, "she did so out of innate good manners and a desire to put herself in the shoes of others, which is one of her more endearing qualities."

The crowds, who waited for hours in the punishing weather to greet the royal couple, were enchanted by Diana's ability to make them feel important. Her natural style of communication—clasping people's hands and thanking them for coming out to see her—melted many Welsh hearts. And when Diana delivered part of a speech at Cardiff City Hall in Welsh, the event was the crowning touch to a triumphant first visit as Princess of Wales.

But Diana was struggling mightily beneath her beaming exterior. "Desperately trying to make [Charles] proud of me" is how she characterized that period of her adjustment to royal life. At first she was terrified by the crowds and needed Charles's encouragement before emerging from their car to mingle. Once she became accustomed to her public duties, though, Diana learned to take her stardom in stride. In *Diana: Her True Story—In Her Own Words*, Andrew Morton describes what happened during that first public appearance in Wales:

> The crowds made it painfully obvious who was the new star of the show—the Princess of Wales. Charles was left apologizing for not having enough wives to go around. If he took one side of the street during a walk-about the crowd collectively groaned, it was his wife they had come to see.

In a 1995 interview, Diana reflected upon the phenomenon she had become after her marriage. "I was very daunted because as far as I was concerned I was a fat, chubby, 20-year-old . . . and I couldn't understand the level of interest." The royal family, including Diana, had assumed that the media's fascination with her would subside after the wedding. But it didn't. Instead, Charles found himself trailing his wife whenever they made appearances together and collecting flowers meant for her. Diana would later lament that she and her husband were once "a very good team," but this opinion was probably not shared by Prince Charles, whose personality was eclipsed by his young bride's charm and appeal.

Charles's growing resentment of Diana was not entirely unfounded. Never a scholar, Diana stubbornly refused to prepare for her public appearances. Her private secretary, Oliver Everett, painstakingly prepared information packets about places, people, and institutions she was scheduled to visit. Diana was expected to study them—just as all the other royals did—so that she could hold informed conversations during official engagements. Everett tried in vain to accommodate the obstinate young princess by breaking the information down to the simplest facts and figures. But the packets usually sat untouched on Diana's desk. She relied instead on her megawatt smile, energy, and fashion sense to carry her through public appearances.

Diana, who had always chafed at being told what to do, felt unfairly burdened by the added pressure of "homework." Charles, meanwhile, bristled at what he saw as laziness and immaturity. Although in later years Diana's preparedness would elicit praise from the many charitable organizations she worked with, her improved study habits were slow to develop.

After Diana's pregnancy was announced on November 5, 1981, she received a brief reprieve from a full schedule of activities. Since the nausea and vomiting that plague many women in early pregnancy persisted in her case, she was assigned less demanding appearances such as hosting a Christmas lighting ceremony on London's Regent Street. She later recalled bolting from the table during many a formal dinner at Windsor Castle—to the obvious exasperation of the other royals—because she felt sick. Still, Diana refused to stop attending formal engagements. She felt torn between forgoing the dinners and being accused of shirking her duty or being sick and creating an embarrassing spectacle in the eyes of her in-laws.

Diana's sense of feeling trapped went beyond a fear of censure at dinner, however. She began to inflict injuries upon herself to release the tension, acting on impulses that had begun to grip her during her honeymoon with Charles. Mental health experts disagree on whether self-mutilation is an illness in itself or is symptomatic of other psychiatric disorders. Self-inflicted injuries can range from slashing one's skin—as Diana often did—to amputating one's limbs or blinding oneself in the most severe cases. Some evidence suggests that self-mutilators also tend to be perfectionists, to feel a deep sense of rejection, and to suffer from eating disorders. "When no one listens to you, or you feel no one's listening to you," Diana later said of her own struggles with self-

*The Prince and Princess of Wales in a family photo with eight-month-old Prince William (nicknamed "Wills"), at Kensington Palace, February 1983.*

mutilation, "all sorts of things start to happen."

All sorts of things did indeed start happening to Diana—injuries of her own making. In January 1982, when the couple was staying at Sandringham, next to Diana's childhood home, Diana tearfully begged Charles for help in adapting to the demands of royal life. Irritated by his wife's continual distress, Charles stomped off to go riding. Diana threw herself down a staircase. A physical exam revealed bruises but no harm to her unborn baby. Charles remained unmoved: "just dismissal, total dismissal," she said of her husband's response to her alarming behavior.

Andrew Morton described other desperate attempts by Diana to draw attention to her plight:

On one occasion she threw herself against a glass display cabinet at Kensington Palace while on another she slashed her wrists with a razor blade. Another time she cut herself with the serrated edge of a lemon slicer; on yet another occasion, during a heated argument with Prince Charles, she picked up a penknife lying on his dressing table and cut her chest and her thighs. Although she was bleeding her husband studiously scorned her. As ever he thought that she was faking her problems.

Even as Diana displayed this extremely abnormal behavior and repeatedly asked Charles for support, she was left to fend for herself. The queen did take the unprecedented step of asking the press to leave Diana alone as she awaited her child's birth. But the request fell on deaf ears, and Diana was photographed and followed as much as ever. She busied herself with sporadic official appearances and with redecorating her new homes—a suite of more than 25 rooms in London's Kensington Palace, and Highgrove, a country estate in Gloucestershire. Outside Kensington Palace, oddsmakers bet untold amounts of money on the gender of the future heir to the throne. As her pregnancy progressed, "it was as if everybody was monitoring every day for me," she remembered.

Approximately two weeks before her due date, Diana decided to have her labor induced. At 9:30 P.M. on Monday, June 21, 1982, she and Prince Charles became the proud parents of a 7-pound, 10-ounce boy. The first visitors to greet Baby Wales the next morning were Diana's mother, Frances, and her sister Lady Jane Fellowes. The queen was next into the Lindo Wing of St. Mary's Hospital in Paddington. She indulged in a rare moment of humor when she expressed her relief to the crowd outside that the baby had not inherited his father's ears.

By 6:00 on Tuesday evening, Diana decided that she was ready to leave St. Mary's. As the prince and princess emerged to greet their public, with Diana cradling their tightly swaddled son, they showed no evidence of marital strife. Still, they disagreed on what to call Baby Wales. Charles voted for "Arthur"; Diana held out for "William." For the first week of his life, Diana's son went unnamed—just as she had after her birth. Diana's strong will eventually prevailed, and William Arthur Philip Louis was christened on Wednesday, August 4, 1982. "Endless pictures of the Queen, Queen Mother, Charles and William," she remembered. "I was excluded totally that day."

A malady known as postpartum depression, which affects some women who have recently given birth, was coloring Diana's perceptions. The journey from living in near obscurity to being the mother of the future king of England drained her: "One minute I was nobody, the next minute I was Princess of Wales, mother, media toy, member of this family, you name it, and it was too much for one person at that time." She had learned not to expect sympathy from her husband and in-laws. They wanted her to keep the proverbial stiff upper lip, both in public and in private. "Well maybe I was the first person . . . in this family who ever had a depression or was ever openly tearful," Diana later said, describing the royal family's impatience with her. "And obviously that was daunting, because if you've never seen [that behavior] before how do you support it?"

Although Charles seemed to avoid displays of normal human emotion with Diana, he proved an affectionate father to Prince William. Their son's arrival brought the couple together for a time; the two shared few other interests, but both were obsessed with the baby they nicknamed Wills. Although they relied on nanny Barbara Barnes when their royal duties called, the princess and the prince broke with royal tradition by assuming a great deal of William's care.

Perhaps this upswing in her marriage gave Diana the confidence to speak up on her own behalf. In September

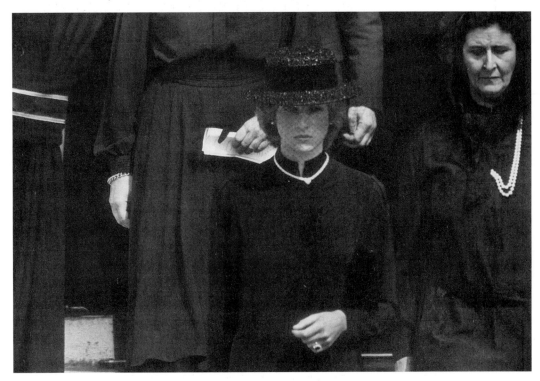

1982, Princess Grace of Monaco was killed in an auto-mobile accident. Diana had a special reason for wanting to attend the princess's funeral: it was Princess Grace who had put 19-year-old Diana at ease on the night Diana made her public debut in the infamous black dress. The mature and experienced princess of Monaco had consoled the young, terrified woman who was about to become a princess herself. So when the queen's secretary refused Diana's written request to attend the funeral, she went directly to the queen herself. Diana's poised presence at Princess Grace's funeral made this first solo journey on behalf of the royal family a success.

This determination carried over to her baby's care. "He's not hidden upstairs with the governess," she would later say of William's upbringing. This was a departure from Charles's childhood: according to some sources, Queen Elizabeth II spent about 30 minutes a day with her eldest son when he was a child.

*Diana appealed directly to Queen Elizabeth for permission to attend the funeral of Princess Grace of Monaco, who was killed in a car accident in September 1982. The sad occasion marked Diana's first time alone representing the British royal family abroad.*

*Toddler Prince Harry (left) arrives in Scotland with his mother and brother to visit Prince Charles at Balmoral in October 1986. According to Diana, shortly after Harry's birth in 1984 her marriage "went down the drain."*

So insistent was Diana on being with her son as much as possible that she took Wills along on her first major overseas tour with Charles to Australia in March and April 1983. When Malcolm Fraser, then prime minister of Australia, learned of Diana's wish to travel with her son, he arranged for Wills and Barbara Barnes to stay at a sheep farm in New South Wales while Diana and Charles fulfilled their duties. "While his parents could only be with him during the occasional break in a hectic schedule," Andrew Morton wrote, "at least Diana knew that he was under the same skies."

The sun often blazed mercilessly in the skies above Australia and New Zealand, but Diana discovered that the blistering heat didn't deter crowds from surrounding them wherever she and her husband went. As in Wales in 1981, however, people really wanted to see her, not Charles. She was distressed not only at being "the one who was always pitched out front," mobbed, and photographed "whether it was my clothes, what I said, what my hair was doing, everything," but also because she and Charles "wanted to be . . . a team" yet were not recognized by the public as such. The public's clear preference for Charles's vibrant, stylish young wife irked him and made him resentful.

When the royal couple returned to England, Diana recalled in 1995, "I was a different person. I realized the sense of duty, the level of intensity of interest, and the demanding role I now found myself in." Though she became a polished performer after the successful six-week tour, her private demons were still very much alive. The princess's bulimia remained out of control. The royal family's failure to acknowledge her triumphs as she struggled to fit in made her illness worse. "Well, anything good I ever did, nobody ever said a thing," she recalled of life after that first overseas tour. "But if I tripped up, which invariably I did, because I was new at the game, a ton of bricks came down on me."

The visit to Australia and New Zealand also marked the end of the happy interlude that had begun with Prince William's birth. Diana later claimed that Charles was fully aware of her bulimia by this time; instead of offering support, he allegedly made snide remarks to his wife about the wastefulness of eating food only to throw it up again. The press merrily amplified whispered rumors of the gaunt-looking princess's eating disorder. Soon after the Australia–New Zealand tour, while Diana was still struggling with depression, the press turned full circle on its star attraction. Negative stories surfaced about Diana's runaway spending on clothes. The young woman who became engaged owning only "one long dress, one silk shirt, [and] one smart

*Although Diana got along very well with Edward Adeane (above), Charles's private secretary and treasurer, the press blamed her for his 1985 resignation and for the high turnover of royal staff members after the prince's marriage.*

pair of shoes" had become an international trendsetter. She was the owner of dozens of custom-tailored evening gowns, suits and dresses, shoes, hats, and handbags. The spendthrift label stung Diana—especially because the same people who criticized her also expected her to be a dazzling paragon of style. Tall, slim, and poised, Diana was courted by fashion designers who wanted her to wear their creations. Now, however, the very clothing that she was tacitly expected to wear made her a target for negative publicity.

The criticism continued. "She was no longer the fairytale Princess but the royal shopaholic who lavished a fortune on an endless array of new outfits. It was Diana who was held responsible for the steady stream of royal staff who had left their service during the previous 18 months and it was the Princess who was accused of forcing Charles to abandon his friends, change his eating habits and his wardrobe," Andrew Morton wrote. When Edward Adeane, Prince Charles's private secretary, resigned after years of serving the royal family, the princess was blamed. She hotly denied any responsibility for his departure. Unfortunately, however, her vehemence only fueled press speculation that she had driven Adeane away.

Diana also maintained that the prince made his own decisions about his diet and lifestyle. She had been taken to task in the early 1980s for persuading Charles to become a vegetarian. It is not hard to imagine that Charles would have made these decisions on his own. Moreover, the prince's former bodyguard, Paul Officer, was a vegetarian and was known to have persuaded Charles to adopt a non-meat diet. And while Diana did occasionally give Charles gifts of clothing or offer an opinion on his style of dress, he was nearly 13 years her senior and had definite tastes of his own.

As for Charles's friends, Diana had always felt out of place among what she called "The Highgrove Set"— fawning admirers of the prince who joined him at their country home for outdoor pursuits that held little interest for Diana. One of the Highgrove set was Camilla Parker-Bowles, and Diana still feared that Charles was secretly seeing her.

The renewed warmth between Charles and Diana as they awaited their second child momentarily calmed her fears, however. Prince Henry (nicknamed Harry) made his debut at 4:20 P.M. on Saturday, September 15, 1984, at St. Mary's Hospital. "We were very, very close to each other the six weeks before Harry was born," she said later. Charles was solicitous of his wife during her second pregnancy and hoped for a girl. Diana kept a secret from him, though: she already knew she was carrying a boy, thanks to a sonogram reading.

The prince did nothing to conceal his disappointment upon the birth of another son. According to Diana, the marriage abruptly "went down the drain." According to the prince, not only was the baby the wrong gender but he was also flawed by red hair. Charles went so far as to complain about his new son's shortcomings to Diana's mother at the christening. Frances Shand Kydd sharply rebuked Prince Charles, admonishing him to be thankful for a healthy child, male or female.

Charles soon grew to love the cheerful, impish little Prince Harry. But for Diana, his affections were too little and too late. "Something inside me closed off," she remembered. At just 23 years old, she had captured the world's imagination, then floundered under the weight of public scrutiny and criticism. She had married a prince only to end up bitterly disenchanted. Although she relished being a mother, life in the public eye and the binge-purge cycle of bulimia in which she was ensnared sapped her energy. Her Royal Highness Diana, Princess of Wales, had become an international star—but at great cost.

*Even as her health worsened and her marriage to Charles deteriorated, Princess Diana appeared to become more at ease during public appearances. Here she greets well-wishers in Atherstone, Warwickshire, in 1985.*

# 7

# "I'D MUCH RATHER BE DOING SOMETHING USEFUL"

*"I think the British people need someone in public life to give affection, to make them feel important, to give them light in dark tunnels."*

—Princess Diana during a 1995 BBC-TV interview

Diana tried to cope with her deteriorating marriage by concentrating on other things, as she had done as a child when her parents divorced. Princes William and Harry were her top priority. She made sure that her schedule matched theirs as closely as possible, charting their events in her date book with green ink. Although rumors about Diana's compromised physical and emotional health abounded, the joy she took in her sons was obvious.

Diana also tried to escape her private misery by playing matchmaker for her friend Sarah Ferguson. A distant cousin of Diana's, Sarah was slightly older and more worldly than the princess. But the two women had much in common. Sarah's parents divorced when she was 14 years old; her mother, Susan, left Major Ronald Ferguson for an Argentinean polo player named Hector Barrantes. Like Diana, Sarah was linked to the royals through her father, who was Prince Charles's polo manager. And Sarah was well known among her friends for her playfulness, just as Diana had been before her mischievous streak was buried under the weight of her shattered dreams and pervasive bulimia.

The high spirits of "Fergie" buoyed Diana during her first pregnancy. The ebullient, redheaded Sarah paid frequent visits to Diana, whom she addressed by her childhood nickname "Duch." Diana returned the favor by introducing Fergie to one of her oldest friends, her brother-in-law Prince Andrew, the duke of York.

When a romance between Sarah Ferguson and Prince Andrew grew into an engagement, Diana finally felt she had a confidante in the royal family's inner circle. She attempted to show the loud, boisterous Fergie how to navigate such treacherous social terrain as visiting Balmoral and behaving in public with the subdued grace expected of a royal wife. Fergie, in turn, helped Diana rediscover her own sense of humor. One of their capers was to disguise themselves as policewomen on the night of Prince Andrew's bachelor party, intending to crash the party in their getups. But they managed only to stop Andrew's car at the gates of Buckingham Palace after the festivities had ended.

Diana was especially grateful for Fergie's companionship because she felt that Charles was trying to isolate her. Shortly before Sarah and Andrew's wedding on July 23, 1986, Sergeant Barry Mannakee, Diana's bodyguard and friend, was transferred to other duties.

Since the night she was escorted from 60 Coleherne Court to Clarence House before her own wedding, Diana had never traveled alone. Even though she despised the idea of being shadowed by bodyguards, the princess had formed friendships with the officers assigned to protect her. She bought them presents at Christmas; she confided in them when she felt misunderstood. Because Mannakee had provided a particularly sympathetic ear, Diana couldn't help suspecting that

Charles had deliberately sent her friend away. She was devastated when Mannakee died in a motorcycle accident less than a year later.

Despite her sorrows, Diana—along with most of Great Britain—was caught up in the levity that Sarah added to the royal routine. The princess and the newly wed duchess of York carried on more like two giggly girlfriends than members of the monarchy. When they were captured on camera poking a friend in the backside with their umbrellas at the Ascot races, the queen dressed them down for their lack of decorum. Diana took the lesson to heart and began to distance herself from Fergie's antics.

*Diana gained a new confi- dante when Sarah Ferguson became a member of the royal family in 1986.*

Understandably, Diana and Sarah's relationship eventually developed a competitive edge. "I got terribly jealous and she got terribly jealous of me," Diana admitted. The princess found herself in the shadow of her sporty, outgoing sister-in-law, invariably coming up short in comparison. After all, as Andrew Morton wrote, Sarah "displayed enthusiasm where Diana showed dismay, hearty jollity compared with Diana's droopy silences and boundless energy against the Princess's constant illness." Long before Sarah Ferguson married Charles's brother, the prince had begun making disparaging comparisons between his depressed wife and the effervescent Fergie.

Perhaps it was Diana's desire to prove him wrong that led to her bravura dance performance on December 23, 1985. She began that evening seated next to her husband in the royal box as they watched a benefit performance at the Royal Opera House in Covent Garden. After sitting quietly through most of the program, Diana excused herself to trade her red velvet gown for a slinky off-white satin dance dress. When the curtain came up for the final number of the night, there stood Diana, partnered with dancer and choreographer Wayne Sleep. The astonished crowd delighted in every step of their four-minute routine, set to Billy Joel's song "Uptown Girl." Sleep, with whom Diana had been secretly rehearsing, later described lifting her across the stage as "comical," since she was a full nine inches taller than he is. The dancing princess beamed with every step, dropping a curtsy to her stunned husband when she finished.

"I think Charles was surprised by what she could do, because she was dancing extremely well," said Reg Wilson, a photographer who covered the benefit. According to Diana, however, the prince's private reaction was less than enthusiastic. He considered her showstopping performance flashy and undignified. "No matter how hard she tried or what she did," wrote Andrew Morton, "every time she struggled to express something of herself, he crushed her spirit."

Diana soon stopped trying altogether. Her bulimia worsened. Speculation about Diana's eating habits had increased shortly after William's birth; she was pronounced anorexic or bulimic countless times in the pages of England's tabloids. Although the Palace tried to keep her condition a secret, it became shockingly clear that Diana was unwell after she fainted during a visit to Vancouver. She was there to open the Expo—a fair featuring exhibits from around the world—when she leaned against her husband and whispered, "Darling, I think I'm about to disappear," before sliding to the ground.

"My husband told me off," Diana recounted of the prince's reaction to the episode. "He said I could have passed out quietly somewhere else, behind a door." Although a superstar to her admirers, she was still regarded as a problematic, somewhat embarrassing figure by the royal family.

Diana felt lost in a world of pain that she could not have anticipated on that beautiful July day in 1981 when she became Her Royal Highness, the Princess of Wales. Her efforts to just "be Diana" had backfired miserably; so had her attempts to imitate Fergie. Beneath Diana's self-pity and suffering, however, a kernel of strength remained. It was up to her to summon that strength and reclaim her own identity.

A ski trip to Klosters, Switzerland, in 1988 turned into a surprising demonstration of Diana's ability to take charge in a crisis. A bout of influenza kept Diana off the slopes on the afternoon of March 10. Fergie, four months pregnant and recuperating from a minor skiing accident, was in the chalet with her when a royal aide named Philip Mackie told them that there had been an avalanche and that one of their party—which included Charles—had been killed. When Charles phoned the chalet to assure them he was all right, he

*As she had done at Princess Grace's funeral, Diana demonstrated remarkable strength and compassion after an avalanche took the life of Major Hugh Lindsay in 1988. "I felt terribly in charge of the whole thing," she said, describing her efforts to escort Lindsay's body home to his widow.*

told Diana and Sarah that Major Hugh Lindsay, a former equerry to the queen, was dead.

"That really turned me inside out," the princess later recalled. Diana was grief-stricken not only for Hugh but also for his new wife, Sarah, who was expecting the Lindsays' first child. Diana snapped into action, ordering Fergie to help her pack Hugh's belongings for Sarah Lindsay. She sent her guard to get the body from the hospital. "I felt terribly in charge of the whole thing," she said later. Charles argued against cutting the trip short, but Diana put her foot down. She felt personally obligated to take Major Lindsay's body home to his widow.

After their return, Diana invited Sarah Lindsay to stay with her at Highgrove for a few days. The princess's sister, Lady Jane Fellowes, joined them. Diana had successfully stood up to Prince Charles—and had spared the monarchy from appearing frivolous and cold-blooded in the bargain. In *Diana: Her True Story—In Her Own Words*, Andrew Morton described Diana's small victory at Klosters as "the beginning of the slow process of awakening to the qualities and possibilities which lay within herself."

But the process that Morton described was actually more of a reawakening. Even as a child the princess had possessed an extraordinary capacity for helping others, sometimes to the point of being bossy. Diana herself was now in need of a little bossing, however. Carolyn Bartholomew had worried about her old friend's health ever since the engagement to Charles. She knew how serious Diana's eating disorder had become and was determined to save her, regardless of the royal family's desire to avoid embarrassment. In 1988, Carolyn telephoned Diana and threatened to spill the details of her bulimia to the press if she did not get help. Diana was shaken enough to comply.

She turned to Dr. Maurice Lipsedge, who had helped her sister Sarah conquer anorexia nervosa a

*Charles and Diana with five-year-old Wills and two-year-old Harry during a family holiday in Palma de Mallorca, Spain, 1987. Though Diana knew that Charles was a very good father, she was troubled by his inability to be openly affectionate with his sons.*

decade earlier. Therapist and patient established an instant rapport, although recovery proved a long, difficult process. By the early 1990s, Diana publicly confessed to "lots of odd bursts" of self-induced vomiting. Although she was far from completely cured, this was a remarkable improvement from the four or so episodes a day that had once seriously threatened her health.

Despite her personal frailties, Diana had never

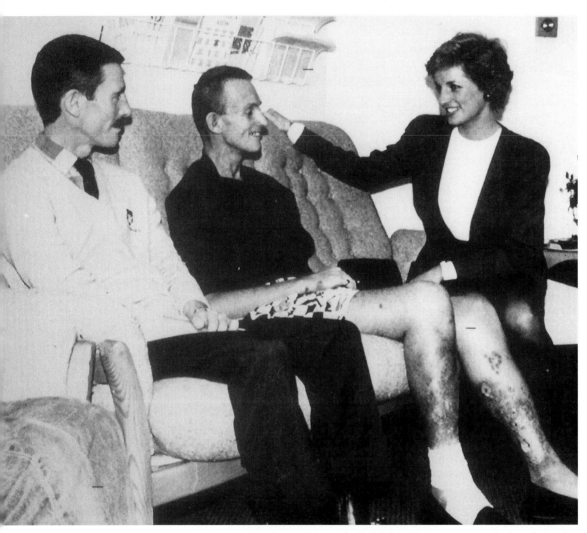

*Diana's willingness to embrace challenging and unpopular causes such as AIDS patient care stemmed from her deep desire to help the sick feel loved and wanted. Here she visits two AIDS sufferers at St. Mary's Hospital in London in 1989.*

relented in her crusade to raise her sons to understand people from all walks of life. Flouting the royal family's tradition of private schooling in the palace nursery, Diana insisted that her sons attend school with other children. The boys' primary school, London's Wetherby School, offered them a chance to interact with their peers before heading off to boarding school. Diana had overruled Prince Charles on this matter. It was her mission to give Great Britain what the media called "an heir and a spare" who would understand life both outside and inside palace walls.

Although the princess knew that her increasingly estranged husband loved his children, she was distressed by Charles's inability to openly demonstrate concern and affection. The press shared Diana's dismay in June 1991, when Prince William suffered a skull fracture after a classmate accidentally hit him on the head with a golf club. After initial tests at the Royal Berkshire Hospital, William's doctors transferred him to London's Great Ormond Street Hospital for Sick Children. Both parents made the journey with him, Diana in the ambulance and Charles following in his car.

After listening to the doctors' recommendation—immediate surgery—Prince Charles decided to stick to his itinerary, which included taking a group of European Union representatives to an evening of opera at Covent Garden, followed by an overnight trip to North Yorkshire for an environmental conference the next day. Although William's surgery was a short procedure, it did pose a slight risk of permanent brain damage. Diana waited alone outside the operating room for 75 agonizing minutes until neurosurgeon Richard Hayward successfully completed the operation. She held Prince William's hand through the night, saddened but not surprised by her husband's seeming indifference to his son's condition.

The public, on the other hand, was stunned. Tabloid headlines screamed of Charles's absentee fathering and took note of Diana's bedside vigil. She was now the popular embodiment of scorned love and maternal devotion. The sensationalist reports dovetailed with the princess's evident personal growth and restored Diana, Princess of Wales, to her former place in the heart of the British people.

As Diana matured, she was no longer content to promote frivolous or lightweight causes. She took the unprecedented step of using her royal status to champion the forsaken and the downtrodden. Although one cannot "catch" AIDS through casual contact, some Britons were shocked and horrified when Diana extended her bare hand to touch a young man dying from AIDS complications at the 1987 opening of London's first treatment center devoted exclusively to the disease. Her gesture struck a wrong note with Prince Charles, who considered AIDS an inappropriate cause for royal attention, and with a few ultra-conservatives who dubbed her "the patron saint of sodomy." But many were moved by Diana's fearless compassion at a time when most people's understanding about the transmission of HIV was still murky.

Diana's commitment to AIDS patients transcended her public visits to hospices and clinics, though. In 1991, she would disobey the queen to be at the bedside of her friend, art dealer Adrian Ward-Jackson, who was dying of complications from the disease. As patron of the Royal Ballet, she had met Ward-Jackson through his work on the company's board. There she had also met and befriended Angela Serota, a former Royal Ballet dancer who now cared for Ward-Jackson in his Mayfair apartment as his life ebbed away.

As she grew closer to Adrian and Angela, Diana brought Princes William and Harry to visit. She once explained her practice of taking the boys to sickrooms, hospices, and homeless shelters by saying, "I want them to have an understanding of people's emotions, people's insecurities, people's distress, and people's hopes and dreams."

In August of 1991, Adrian Ward-Jackson was admitted to St. Mary's Hospital in Paddington to spend his final days. But Diana was expected to fly to Italy and join her family on a Mediterranean cruise. She reluctantly went, later departing the ship by helicopter to rush back to Ward-Jackson's bedside. On the 19th, the end was closing in, and Diana was again away—this time at Balmoral. That evening, she made the 600-mile drive from the Scottish castle to London to see her

friend, having left Balmoral without the queen's permission. The rest of the royal family could not understand why Diana would want to make more than brief,
occasional visits to Ward-Jackson.

Diana's dear friend lingered between life and death
until August 23. For three days, Diana spent most of
her waking hours at the hospital—in direct defiance of
the queen's orders that she return to Balmoral. During
her vigil, the princess also managed to comfort the family of a woman who had undergone heart surgery and
died suddenly, as her children and other relatives
watched helplessly. Diana kept the family company
while they struggled with their initial shock and grief.

After Adrian Ward-Jackson died, Diana insisted that
Angela Serota accompany her when she joined her family in France. During Adrian's funeral at St. Paul's
Church in Knightsbridge, however, the rigid codes of
royal behavior separated Diana and Angela: the princess
had to sit on the right side of the church, which was
strictly reserved for royalty.

The kindness Diana displayed at St. Mary's Hospital
during those draining days was not an isolated inci-
dent. She made spontaneous visits whenever she
sensed that she could help someone overcome his or
her troubles. In 1987, she had delighted a young boy
named Shaun Barford—the son of Bridget Barford, a
cleaning woman at Althorp House—with a visit to his
London hospital room where he lay dying of cystic
fibrosis. In 1990, while visiting Prince Charles in the
hospital as he recovered from a broken right arm,
Diana made time to visit patients in the intensive care
unit. The satisfaction she felt in privately comforting
others countered the conjectures of some of her critics
that she was merely a publicity junkie who exploited
the suffering of others.

As she found meaning in helping others, Diana's
interests changed. She no longer felt comfortable sitting in the royal box at the Ascot races or attending

*The Prince and Princess of Wales visited South Korea in November 1992 on what was dubbed a "togetherness tour." A month later, their separation was announced. "We'd struggled to keep [the marriage] going," Diana later said, "but . . . we'd both run out of steam."*

frivolous parties. "I'd much rather be doing something useful," she remarked.

But the royal family often disagreed with Diana's definition of useful work. Her interest in AIDS patients, the homeless, battered women, and people with leprosy was considered distasteful by Prince Charles. Nor did the royals approve of her practice of taking Princes William and Harry with her on visits to shelters and clinics. The concerns of the wildly popular princess directly challenged those of Charles, whose interests in the environment and architecture seemed hopelessly irrelevant by comparison.

For the first time, Diana began seriously considering

disentangling herself from Prince Charles, the queen, and their courtiers—whom she referred to as the "grey men." Fergie had already left the royal fold; on March 19, 1992, Buckingham Palace announced Sarah's separation from Prince Andrew. Though Diana was disheartened by the loss of the only other "outsider" in the palace, she was still shrewd enough to distance herself from Sarah and the excessive spending, frequent holidays, and public gaffes that seemed to characterize the duchess at the time. The princess dreaded divorce, but the alternative—wasting her life in a loveless marriage—was equally grim.

The separation of the duke and duchess of York was disgraceful enough to the royals; for the Prince and Princess of Wales, a split was still unthinkable. "It seemed as though the Waleses were headed for the kind of marriage of convenience so common in upper-crust British society," wrote Barbara Kantrowitz. "It was assumed that they would lead essentially separate lives, appearing proper and polite in public."

But the events of 1992 eroded the royal couple's veneer of calm civility. On March 29 Diana's father, Johnnie Spencer, died. Diana grudgingly followed the queen's orders to let Charles accompany her home from a ski vacation in Austria. When they reached Kensington Palace, however, Charles departed for Highgrove without her, reappearing only to attend Earl Spencer's funeral.

The publication of Andrew Morton's book *Diana: Her True Story* in June deepened the rift between Charles and Diana. The book chronicled the princess's pain over Charles's affair with Camilla Parker-Bowles and candidly discussed her attempts to hurt herself and her longtime struggle with bulimia. While she denied ever speaking to Morton herself, Diana admitted that she allowed her friends to talk openly with him. She later explained her reasons for cooperating with a book that was critical of Prince Charles and the monarchy: "I think I was so fed up with being seen as someone who was a basket-case, because I am a very strong person and I know that causes complications in the system that I live in."

But the immediate fallout from Morton's book further complicated her life. First was the reaction of the royal family, which Diana described as "shocked and horrified and very disappointed." The book also hastened the decline of her marriage to Charles, because their soured union "became out in the open and was spoken about on a daily basis." For the image-conscious House of Windsor, this kind of public disclosure was unbearable.

As the Palace's resentment of Diana grew and public pressure intensified for the Waleses either to reconcile or separate, the strain took its toll on the princess. Shortly after the book's release, Diana broke down in tears during a public appearance.

The strain increased on August 25, when the *Sun*, a tabloid newspaper, ran an abridged transcript of a 1989 telephone conversation between Diana and her old friend James Gilbey. During the talk, Diana unburdened herself to Gilbey about the loneliness of royal life and described her marriage as "torture," while Gilbey professed his affection for the princess: "I love you, love you, love you." Newswires blazed with allegations that Diana and Gilbey had carried on an adulterous affair. Because he addressed her by the ridiculous nickname "Squidgy" approximately 15 times during their exchange, reporters dubbed the resulting scandal "Squidgygate."

The *Sun* also opened a telephone hotline where callers could listen to the "Squidgy tape" for a price. Although the tape was allegedly procured by a radio hacker anxious to make money, a mortified Diana sensed that its release was the work of palace insiders attempting to tarnish her image. She later admitted that the taped conversation was authentic, describing Gilbey

as "a very affectionate person," but she denied having had a sexual relationship with him.

Royal biographer Anthony Holden supports Diana's story. "The very naivete of the rambling, teenage dialogue seemed in itself to clear the pair of anything untoward." He also reaffirms her suspicions about the tape's source: "Technical experts on both sides of the Atlantic testified that a recording so sophisticated—Gilbey was speaking from a carphone—could only have been an inside job. But who was trying to discredit Diana, and why?"

In any event, Diana emerged from Squidgygate embarrassed but still loved by millions of people. Even curious hotline callers came to pity her, because her obvious sadness was captured on the tape. But Queen Elizabeth had tired of what she saw as Diana's public

*The role Diana prized most was that of mother to William and Harry. She was determined to expose them to a world beyond royal strictures and duty. Here, mother and sons enjoy a ride on the* Maid of the Mist *at Niagara Falls, Ontario, Canada.*

airing of royal dirty laundry. To appease the queen, the princess reconsidered an earlier decision and joined Prince Charles on an official visit to Korea that fall.

The palace press office put a positive spin on the "togetherness tour," which took place during the first week of November. They billed it as a reconciliation between Charles and Diana. Yet it could not have been further from the truth: Diana's expressive blue eyes and wistful head tilt made her appear sullen and forlorn throughout the trip. She was refusing to cooperate with the Palace's facade of marital harmony, and she no longer cared who noticed. Prince Charles's performance was similarly unconvincing. "If they were still hiding the fact that they couldn't bear to be in the same room together, it was quite clear they couldn't bear to be in the same country," cracked one writer.

The couple's obvious failure to settle their differences while in Korea pointed toward a separation. The final blow to the marriage was the *Daily Mirror*'s revelation that it had a "Camillagate" tape—a racy phone conversation recorded between the prince and Camilla Parker-Bowles. As a result, the royal family became the subject of jokes yet again in 1992. That same year, Windsor Castle caught fire and nearly burned down. Even worse, the date of the fire, November 20, was the 45th wedding anniversary of Queen Elizabeth II and Prince Philip.

By this time, Her Royal Highness, Diana, Princess of Wales, was ready to give up her role in the royal soap opera. The prospect of one day becoming the queen of England no longer mattered to her. On December 9, 1992, British prime minister John Major announced that Prince Charles and Princess Diana had agreed upon an "amicable" separation.

Only two things mattered to Diana now: her work and her sons. Would she be able to continue supporting the causes that gave her life meaning? More important, what would her future role in the lives of Wills and

Harry be? Would she be marginalized by the royal family as they pulled the boys deeper into the world of duty and tradition? "The fairy tale had come to an end," Diana would later say. Now she prepared for whatever lay ahead with equal measures of fear and hope.

*Diana on her own: in January 1997, the princess visited Angola in an effort to raise awareness of the devastation of land mines. She is shown here delivering a speech at the Luanda International Airport upon her arrival.*

# 8

# SAFER
# BY HERSELF

*"I've got things to do and time is precious."*

—Princess Diana, in an interview
with Andrew Morton, 1995

With profound sadness, Princess Diana repeated for her sons the history of the broken marriage that had marred her own childhood. She was determined to soften as much as possible the blow of her separation from their father. A week before the public announcement of their split, Diana journeyed to Ludgrove School to break the news to Harry and Wills. Inwardly stung by Charles's love for Camilla Parker-Bowles, she was nonetheless careful not to mention his adultery to her sons. Diana had never forgotten the scandal surrounding her mother's departure from Park House some 25 years earlier. She did her best to spare her own children the helpless confusion she had felt then.

But Diana also had those feelings in the present. She knew that her ongoing charity work was now in jeopardy. The royal family had grudgingly tolerated her popularity when she was securely

*"I never know where a lens is going to be," Diana once said of the overwhelming media attention she began receiving from the time of her engagement to Prince Charles. She found the public's keen interest in her "daunting and phenomenal."*

within their ranks. Now that Diana was separated from Charles, she feared that the family would attempt to push her off of the world stage once and for all.

Diana's fear was well founded. Around the time of her formal separation, the princess tried to safeguard her future as a humanitarian. She approached Prime Minister John Major about becoming an official goodwill ambassador for England and the rest of Great Britain. Although Major thought Diana's idea was stellar, he backed down when the royal family squelched the plan.

To make matters worse, Charles's and Diana's respective office staffs still tensely coexisted in St. James Palace. "Well, my husband's side were very busy stopping me," she said in a 1995 interview. When asked how Charles's staff had sabotaged her, the princess cited "visits abroad being blocked . . . things that had come naturally my way being stopped, letters . . . that got lost, and various [other] things."

One particularly bizarre attempt to undermine Diana occurred in March 1993 as she prepared for an official visit to the Asian country of Nepal. Prince Charles treated a small group of editors, wealthy art patrons, and other influential Britons to a champagne party at St. James Palace, where he had been living since the separation. But the royal host never showed up. Instead of rubbing elbows with the prince himself, guests fielded anxious questions from his staff: they wanted feedback on their campaign to present Charles as a concerned, caring monarch. The staffers also loudly predicted that Diana's trip would be a failure. Finally, the meeting deteriorated into a round of disparaging remarks about the princess before "forlornly petering out," according to Anthony Holden.

Diana endured more subtle royal snubs during her five-day tour of Nepal. Upon her arrival in Kathmandu, for instance, the band welcoming her was forbidden to play the British national anthem in her honor.

In April, Diana's response to the tragic murder of two English youths exposed the silly one-upmanship of the Palace's efforts to suppress her. Teenagers Tim Parry and Jonathan Ball died when an IRA bomb exploded at a shopping center in Warrington, Lancashire. Diana requested permission to represent the royal family at the boys' memorial service. The queen refused and sent her husband, Prince Philip, instead. Philip, a man not known for his tenderness, struck most people as an odd choice—especially since Diana had long since proven herself a gentle, comforting presence in sad situations.

Diana put her disappointment aside and called the mothers of the victims instead. "I really want to be there but I can't be," she told Wendy Parry. She expressed her condolences to Maria Ball as well. "She was ever so nice," said Mrs. Parry to reporters. "It gave me a big boost to talk to her."

The story of Diana's condolence calls was thus innocently leaked to the media, and the royal family became incensed. They all but accused Diana of upstaging them. The princess came to regret the furor caused by her sympathetic phone calls, but she was not sorry about offering comfort to the bereaved families.

Diana's early attempts to work harmoniously with the royal family while no longer a full-fledged member were immensely frustrating. A visit to Zimbabwe in July 1993 was the breaking point. She felt that the Palace's expectations of her clashed hopelessly with her own aspirations. In *Diana: Her New Life*, Andrew Morton described a photo opportunity that took place on that visit "where she was pictured doling out food to children like a glorified waitress." The shots "symbolized her deep dissatisfaction with the whole inane circus. She felt the exercise humiliated her, patronized the children, and demeaned the purpose of her visit, by reinforcing the 'begging-bowl' image of Africa. . . . She vowed that it would never happen again."

The summer and fall of 1993 sapped Diana's energy. She was perpetually on the defensive against her estranged husband's attempts to discredit her. More worrisome, however, was Diana's realization that she could not effectively do the work she found most meaningful—comforting the world's forgotten—while struggling on the sidelines of the royal family. Thus, the seemingly defeated Princess of Wales announced her retirement from public life at the London Hilton on December 3.

In the wake of her "time and space speech," Diana's fledgling career of charitable works was in suspension. It was far from over, however: only weeks earlier, she had quietly accepted the presidency of the British Red Cross. During the very first weekend of her "retirement,"

Diana also took time to visit the hospital room of an 11-year-old girl dying of complications from AIDS.

As she lowered her own public profile, Diana faced the prospect of playing a diminished role in her sons' lives. Christmas of 1993 made the princess painfully aware that when it came to seeing her children, she was at the mercy of the royal family. She already knew that her access to them was largely dependent upon her ability to avoid ruffling the queen's feathers. By right of an obscure English legal ruling called the Grand Question, Queen Elizabeth could even take custody of the boys if she saw fit. "In bald terms," wrote Andrew Morton in *Diana: Her New Life*, "the Princess of Wales, universally admired as a caring mother, has fewer rights over her children than a divorcée raising a family in a tenement."

Diana agreed to leave the boys at Her Majesty's country home in Sandringham on Christmas Day. Although she stayed to open presents with William and Harry on Christmas Eve, she spent the next day alone. "I felt so sorry for myself," she later recalled.

At first, both the prince and princess were guilty of playing tug-of-war with William and Harry. Charles took them for a luxury cruise; Diana responded by flying them to Disney World. But despite her petty battles with Charles, Diana was determined to fill their lives with as many normal experiences as possible. Throughout the trip to Disney World, for example, she insisted that they forego VIP treatment and wait in lines with other children.

Particularly upsetting to Diana was Charles's hiring of a young woman named Tiggy Legge-Bourke, a fun-loving nanny who essentially acted as a surrogate mother to the princes when they visited their father. Photographs of Tiggy doing such simple things as buying ice cream for Wills and Harry filled Diana with anger because she feared being replaced in their affections.

Despite the indignities she suffered after separating from Charles, Diana refused to give up public life for long. She resumed her humanitarian role, sticking to the urgent—and in royal circles, controversial—causes she believed in, such as AIDS research and patient care.

The princess's priorities were similarly unwavering when it came to Wills and Harry. She incorporated her philosophies on child-rearing into a speech on AIDS when she said, "I am only too aware of the temptation of avoiding harsh reality; not just for myself but for my own children too. Am I doing them a favor if I hide suffering and unpleasantness from them until the last possible minute?"

Living on her own in the real world also exposed Diana to her share of less-than-fairy-tale situations. On June 29, 1994, the princess made a point of ignoring Jonathan Dimbleby's televised interview with Prince Charles, in which he confessed to conducting a long-term affair with Camilla Parker-Bowles while implying that he had never loved Diana. That October, her sons' former riding teacher, Captain James Hewitt, with help from writer Anna Pasternak, published *Princess in Love*, an exposé of his alleged five-year affair with the princess. In February 1995, she successfully sued a London health club employee named Bryce Taylor for photographing her with a hidden camera as she worked out. In her case against Taylor, Diana unwittingly broke new ground as the first royal of the 20th century to testify in a civil court.

Despite Diana's formal attempt to withdraw from public life nearly two years earlier, she remained the subject of intense media curiosity in 1995. Feeling compelled to set the record straight about her life and her failed marriage, Diana sat for an interview with Martin Bashir of the BBC-TV program *Panorama*. The hour-long interview aired on November 20. The princess openly discussed her bulimia ("just a feeling of being no good at anything and being useless and hopeless and failed in every direction"); Prince Charles and Camilla ("Well, there were three of us in this marriage, so it was a bit crowded"); and her hopes for the future ("I've had difficulties, as everybody has witnessed over the years, but let's now use the knowledge I've gathered to help other people in distress").

When asked about Captain James Hewitt's book, *Princess in Love*, Diana admitted that she and Hewitt had indeed carried on an adulterous affair. "Yes, I was in love with him," she confessed. The princess described herself as "absolutely devastated" by his betrayal when the book came out, and described how she "rushed" to talk to William and Harry about the book's contents so that they would not learn about the affair from other, less sympathetic sources. She also dismissed *Princess in Love* as containing "a lot of fantasy."

She expressed her desire to become a "queen of people's hearts" since becoming queen of England now seemed unlikely. In addition, Diana told Bashir about the importance of exposing her sons—particularly Prince William—to all sides of life, as well as preparing them to face constant ambush by the paparazzi. "There was a relationship which worked before," said Diana of her own dealings with the media, "but now I can't tolerate it because it's become abusive and it's harassment."

Diana's *Panorama* interview caused a sensation in Britain and in America, where parts of it were shown on ABC-TV on November 24. But even the admission of her romance with Hewitt did not dim her international stardom. In fact, the public seemed more sympathetic than ever to Diana, the scorned wife. Her willingness to own up to her weaknesses also endeared her to many

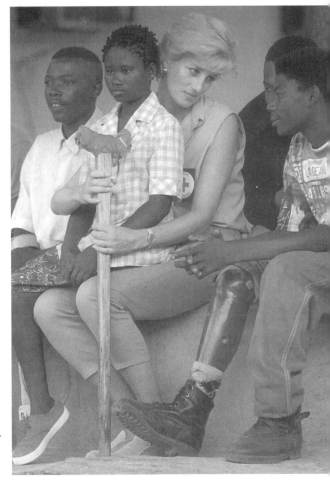

*Representing the British Red Cross, Princess Diana converses with young amputees at an orthopedic hospital in Angola in January 1997. Though she was criticized by a few British politicians as a "loose cannon," Diana wanted to be known not as a political figure but as a humanitarian and goodwill ambassador for Great Britain.*

*For all her troubles with overeager reporters and photographers, Diana learned to use the media to promote the causes and issues she cherished. In 1997, inspired by a suggestion from Prince William, Diana donated 79 gowns from her royal wardrobe to an auction benefitting British and American cancer and AIDS charities. Before the auction, she modeled several of the gowns in the July issue of Vanity Fair.*

people who preferred her warm personal style to the remote coolness of the British royals.

Diana's friend Rosa Monckton says that Diana came to regret doing the interview, however. Monckton described it as "Diana at her worst." The princess did appear nervous and tired on camera, her weary eyes dramatized with heavy black liner. Barbara Walters, a well-known interviewer, had eaten lunch with Diana on the day of the *Panorama* interview. "[S]he had discussed it with her sons," recalled Walters, "and what she cared most about was that she did not want people to think that she was this irresponsible, mentally ill person." Diana need not have worried, however, since her admirers remained loyal even after the interview.

Although during the interview Diana had also expressed her wish to avoid a divorce, she sadly relented and agreed with Charles to begin legal proceedings on February 28, 1996. On August 28, the marriage that had begun with the high hopes of the entire world ended with a coldly worded statement: "[I]t is hereby certified that the said decree was on the 28th day of August 1996 made final and absolute and that the said marriage was thereby dissolved."

Not only did Diana get to stay in Kensington Palace, but the divorce settlement also awarded her £350,000 (roughly $600,000) a year to support her household and office staffs as well as a one-time payment of £17 million (about $26.5 million). But the divorce was costly in terms of Diana's happiness and pride. Although still referred to as the Princess of Wales, she was no longer Her Royal Highness; the divorce decree stripped her of that honorific title. The decree also forbade Diana from taking her sons out of England without the queen's permission—and then only for short periods.

Despite her heartache, Diana was freer than she had ever been in her adult life. She wasted little time in taking on high-profile work with the British Red Cross. In January 1997, she comforted land mine victims in Angola. Although Diana was committed to getting land mines banned in that country, she told a BBC film crew who documented the visit that she had no political agenda. "I want to bring awareness to people in distress, whether it's in Angola or any other part of the world. The fact is, I'm a humanitarian figure," she explained.

In May, Tony Blair replaced John Major as prime minister of Great Britain. Blair openly championed Diana's effort to become a goodwill ambassador abroad, and this time she succeeded. As the divorced Princess of Wales reinvented herself, she also fine-tuned her priorities, reducing the number of organizations that she served as patroness from more than 100 to just six. Of these, only one—the English National Ballet—was not devoted to issues of health or social welfare.

In June 1997, she again toured for the Red Cross in an effort to make the world aware of the dangers of antipersonnel land mines, which maim or kill an estimated 26,000 people each year. She visited Washington, D.C., to raise money for her cause and to discuss it with First Lady Hillary Rodham Clinton. Twelve years earlier, a star-struck young princess had whirled around a White House ballroom on the arm of film star John Travolta during a U.S. tour with Prince Charles. Then, people had expected Diana's ink-blue velvet gown to make a statement; now, people listened to what she had to say.

Since she no longer needed to enthrall an audience with her clothing, Diana decided to clean out her closets for charity. While the princess was in America lobbying against land mines, she also oversaw preparations for a charity auction of 79 gowns she had worn while a member of the royal family. "Yes it is a wrench to let go of these beautiful dresses," Diana said of the auction, which took place on June 25 at Christie's in New York. "However, I am extremely happy that others can now share the joy that I had wearing them."

As she gave away her lavish dresses, the princess took one final bow as an international glamour girl. Before her gowns went to auction, the American magazine *Vanity Fair* persuaded her to model some of them one last time for fashion photographer Mario Testino. Diana smiled from the cover of the July issue, and the photos and article within reflected her newfound confidence and buoyant spirits. "Ultimately they're empty shells—beautiful, shiny, marvelous to look at, but still . . . *shells.* And the fabulous creature who once occupied them? She's packed up and moved on," commented *Vanity Fair* writer Cathy Horyn about Diana and her dresses.

As Diana moved on, she began to explore her spiri-

*Kindred spirits: Mother Teresa (left) and Princess Diana at a New York City Missionaries of Charity residence in June 1997. The two had been friends from the day they met in 1992 in a Rome hospital where Mother Teresa was recovering from a heart condition. They died within a week of one another.*

tuality. While in New York during the summer of 1997, she visited Mother Teresa, who had been a personal friend since their first meeting in 1992. Diana treasured a rosary given to her by the venerated nun and founder of the Sisters of Charity order in Calcutta, India. But the princess also relied on psychic advisors and experimented with healing crystals and New Age books to guide her decisions—practices that prompted Diana's critics to continue calling her frivolous and unstable.

The divorced princess dispensed with many of the trappings of royalty. Although she kept her office staff at St. James Palace, Diana dismissed her ladies-in-waiting and—to the consternation of many observers—her palace security guards. She once said, "I like [life] as normal as possible. Walking along the pavement gives me a tremendous thrill."

But at times Diana seemed to want the best of both a privileged and a private world. On June 21, Diana took Princes William and Harry to the movies at a London cinema to celebrate William's 15th birthday. They saw *The Devil's Own*, an American film starring Brad Pitt and Harrison Ford. It was an unfortunate choice: many Britons were outraged that she took her sons to see a film that they thought glamorized IRA violence. To make matters worse, 12-year-old Prince Harry was too young to see the movie, which was rated suitable for ages 15 and up. Diana begged cinema employees to let Harry stay, knowing they would not dare throw out the Princess of Wales and her children. She issued a public apology in the wake of this embarrassing episode.

The bad press surrounding Diana's blunder was short-lived, and by August she was visiting land-mine victims during a three-day trip to Bosnia. But something overshadowed her rigorous 15-hour days in the crusade for an international ban on land mines.

Diana was in love. What had started as a simple wish to leave England in July—when Charles was slated to host Camilla Parker-Bowles's 50th birthday party at Highgrove—had developed into a summer romance.

She once said of being involved with another person, "I think I am safer alone." Her history with male friends certainly supported that claim. In addition to her role in the 1992 "Squidgygate" scandal and her admitted affair with Captain Hewitt, Diana was also accused of making harassing phone calls to married art dealer Oliver Hoare in 1994 (although the matter was later dropped). In 1995, a British TV personality named Julia Carling blamed Diana for the breakup of her marriage to rugby star Will Carling.

Prince Charles was now openly carrying on a relationship with Camilla, who had divorced Andrew Parker-Bowles in 1995. Although Diana joked with friends about the prospect of popping out of Camilla's birthday cake, she decided instead to take Wills and Harry to visit a Spencer family friend, an Egyptian-born man named Mohamed al-Fayed. They sunned and swam aboard his yacht, the *Jonikal*, in Saint-Tropez, France, as Camilla's birthday bash went on at Highgrove.

During Diana's stay on the *Jonikal*, she met Mohamed's son, Emad, who went by the nickname Dodi. It was not her first encounter with the younger al-Fayed;

*Diana's affection for the young is evident as she chats with Bosnian children during a trip to Bosnia-Herzegovina in August 1997.*

Diana had met Dodi briefly some 10 years earlier when he played polo with Prince Charles. Dodi, 42, was reputed to be something of a playboy. He had one short-lived marriage behind him and previous romantic links to countless glamorous women, among them the American actresses Julia Roberts and Brooke Shields and California model Kelly Fisher—whom he allegedly left to romance Diana. When he wasn't driving one of his five Ferraris around Hollywood, Dodi worked as a film producer. His most famous effort was *Chariots of Fire*, which won the Academy Award for Best Picture in 1981.

His family's dazzling wealth aside, Dodi al-Fayed seemed an unlikely—even inappropriate—match for Diana. His uncle was Adnan Khashoggi, an arms dealer reputed to be one of the wealthiest people in the world. This connection would present an inevitable conflict of interest for a woman who strove to eradicate land mines from the face of the earth.

What was worse in the eyes of British politicians, however, was Diana's visit to Dodi's father in Saint-Tropez. Mohamed al-Fayed had multiplied his fortune by purchasing London's famous Harrods department store, but he was unable to buy what he wanted most: British citizenship. He had attempted to do so several times, though, trying to gain political influence by funding members of Parliament. Diana, who appeared noticeably relaxed and happy on holiday with the al-Fayed family, responded to the resulting criticism by pointing out that the al-Fayeds were old friends of her father and her stepmother, Raine, who was also employed by Harrods.

Diana felt moved to defend her choice of friends to a boat full of British photojournalists who watched her Jet-Ski along the beach in Saint-Tropez. She also asked them to leave William and Harry alone while they were on their vacation. It was Diana's parting words that would reverberate for months to come, however. "Expect a big surprise in the next two weeks," she said as she zoomed away, leaving the bewildered reporters out at sea.

Whatever she had meant, Diana delivered on her promise. Her relationship with Dodi al-Fayed blossomed like a tangle of summer wildflowers. She was thrilled finally to be with someone who was as demonstrative as she was. Dodi openly cuddled and kissed her, uninhibited by the ever-present paparazzi. In fact, a bidding war ensued among the tabloids over a grainy, distant shot of the couple kissing as they cruised the Sardinian coast in Dodi's yacht. "He surrounds me with love and care," she said of the new man in her life. Diana's sons also seemed to like him, according to observers who saw them together at a bistro in Saint-Tropez.

*Diana's romance with Egyptian-born Dodi al-Fayed (left) in the last months of her life aroused frenzied media attention. This photo was taken nine days before the couple's death, as they vacationed in the French Riviera.*

Her last holiday with Dodi began on August 21 after she returned from her visit to Bosnia. In Bosnia, Diana had been disturbed by the press's refusal to focus on the issue at hand; instead, they peppered her with questions about her love affair. Friends say she also wondered whether Dodi took her humanitarian work seriously. Furthermore, according to her confidante Rosa Monckton, Dodi's tendency to give lavishly expensive gifts upset Diana. "That's not what I want, Rosa," the princess told her friend. "It makes me uneasy. I don't want to be bought. I have everything I want. I just want someone to be there for me, to make me feel safe and secure."

Still, gossip was in the air about an imminent wedding. "I haven't taken such a long time to get out of one poor marriage to get into another," Diana told one journalist in an effort to quell the rumors. Whatever the truth might have been, she was clearly having a wonderful time with al-Fayed in late August. They stayed aboard the *Jonikal* until the end of the month. On August 30, Diana and Dodi decided to celebrate a special night in Paris before she returned to England to see her sons.

The couple had been dogged by photographers even as they vacationed on the Mediterranean. But when they arrived at Le Bourget airport outside of Paris, the situation worsened, even though drivers and security guards tried to shield them. Their destination was the al-Fayed-owned Ritz hotel in Paris. Dodi allegedly had purchased a $225,000 diamond ring for Diana while they window-shopped in Monte Carlo, and he planned to present it to her that night. At his luxury apartment on the Champs-Elysées shortly after 7:00 P.M., Diana is believed to have given Dodi two gifts: an inscribed cigar cutter and a pair of cuff links that once belonged to her father.

Their plans for a quiet dinner at a local restaurant had already been squelched, and they decided to return to the Ritz. They arrived there at 9:50, but gawking diners and stalking photographers in the hotel's restaurant drove them upstairs to dine in a private suite.

After midnight, Dodi wanted to go back to his apartment with Diana, according to their original plan. He insisted that driver Henri Paul, the Ritz's deputy of security, come back on duty to take them there. As the crowd of photographers outside the hotel grew, Dodi ordered a decoy car to leave from the front of the Ritz in the hope of luring them away. At 12:20 A.M., Paul drove an armored black Mercedes S-280 away from a rear service entrance with bodyguard Trevor Rees-Jones in the passenger seat and Diana and Dodi in the back. Henri Paul allegedly challenged a group of paparazzi to try and catch them as he peeled out into the night.

Back at his apartment, Dodi had placed a silver plaque engraved with a love poem he had written under Diana's pillow.

She would never read a word of it.

*Princess Diana in Tokyo, Japan, November 1990.*

# 9

# "HOW MANY TIMES SHALL WE REMEMBER HER?"

*Dearest Renee,*

*I wanted you, Manu, and Andre to know that I'm thinking of you so much during this difficult time—I send you all an enormous hug, big kiss, and lots of love.*

—Telegram from Diana to three New Zealand children whose father and sister died at the hands of a drunk driver, received 18 hours after her own death

Diana, Princess of Wales, was pronounced dead at 4:00 A.M. Paris time, Sunday, August 31, 1997, from injuries sustained when the Mercedes in which she was riding struck a pillar in a tunnel underneath Paris's Pont de l'Alma bridge and then slammed into a wall at an estimated speed of about 137 kilometers (85 miles) per hour. The accident happened sometime between 12:35 and 12:49 A.M.

Although La Pitié-Salpêtrière Hospital was only 6½ kilometers (four miles) from the scene of the accident, rescue workers took nearly an hour and a half to free the princess from the wreckage, resuscitate her, and transport her there. Diana's death was appar-

*Above: Angry and grieving, Earl Charles Spencer lashes out at the press following the death of his sister, Diana, on August 31, 1997. Facing page: The princess peers through binoculars to see whether photographers have followed her to a secluded location on Martha's Vineyard in 1994. Decrying the media's relentless pursuit of Diana, Earl Spencer declared, "[My] one consolation is that Diana is now in a place where no human being can ever touch her again."*

ently inevitable no matter how quickly she reached the hospital, however. Her chest had been crushed on impact, causing her to go into cardiac arrest. Surgeons discovered a large wound to her left pulmonary vein— one of the largest and most important veins in the body, carrying oxygenated blood from the lungs to the heart. The leaking pulmonary vein caused such massive blood loss that doctors could not reestablish Diana's circulation. Doctor Bruno Riou, head of intensive care at La Pitié-Salpêtrière, said that his team repaired the vein, then employed "an external and internal cardiac massage lasting two hours" in a valiant attempt to get the princess's blood flowing again.

Before the public announcement of her death came out of La Pitié-Salpêtrière Hospital at 6:00 A.M. Paris time, the fate of Dodi al-Fayed and driver Henri Paul had already been reported. Both men died at the scene of the crash. Bodyguard Trevor Rees-Jones survived, but when he emerged from his coma, Rees-Jones had no memories of the accident that could aid investigators.

Prince Charles, who was at Balmoral with Princes William and Harry, was told of his former wife's death shortly after it happened. Authorities withheld the public announcement of Diana's death for two hours so that Charles could perform the painful task of privately telling his sons the news.

As Charles prepared to fly to Paris and claim Diana's body, Britons who awoke and turned on BBC-TV or BBC radio were greeted by the repeated strains of "God Save the Queen"—and told the shocking news. That morning, Prime Minister Tony Blair's voice broke as he issued a statement about the loss of his friend the princess:

> I feel like everyone else in this country today—utterly devastated. Our thoughts and prayers are with Princess Diana's family—in particular her two sons. . . . We are today a nation in a state of shock, in mourning, in grief that is so deeply painful for us. She was a wonderful and

warm human being. . . . Though her own life was often sadly touched by tragedy, she touched the lives of so many others in Britain and throughout the world with joy and with comfort. How many times shall we remember her, in how many different ways? With the sick, the dying, with children, with the needy—when with just a look or a gesture that spoke so much more than words, she would reveal to all of us the depth of her compassion and her humanity.

Across the Atlantic, Americans were celebrating Labor Day weekend. Television networks were therefore short-staffed and ill-prepared to deliver the torrent of news coverage that this breaking story demanded. As a result, American broadcasters initially relied on feeds from two British networks, Sky News and BBC-TV. Cable News Network (CNN) picked up the story before Diana was declared dead. At first, the condition of the princess was unknown. During this period of grim uncertainty, CNN viewers were surprised by a telephone call to the network from film star Tom Cruise. He bitterly decried the tactics of the paparazzi who had been pursuing Diana and Dodi. Cruise said that he and his wife, actress Nicole Kidman, had been chased through the same tunnel beneath the Pont de l'Alma by photographers on motorcycles. "I think we need laws for what [constitutes] harassing an individual," the actor fumed.

Tom Cruise's incendiary remarks were among the first in an international explosion of rage against the paparazzi—or "stalkarazzi," as they became known. In the wake of the accident, six French photographers and one motorcyclist driving for a press agency were arrested and detained for questioning. They were suspected of having caused the accident by pursuing the Mercedes too closely. On the other hand, Jacques Langevin, one of the photographers being investigated, blamed driver Henri Paul for "zigzagging dangerously," speeding, and running a red light after challenging the paparazzi to catch him. Judge Herve Stephan nonetheless declared all seven photographers official suspects in the case. This meant that they were one step away from criminal charges of involuntary homicide—the French version of manslaughter—and of violating France's "Good Samaritan" law, which states that passersby who fail to help accident victims are criminally liable.

One of the detained photographers, Romuald Rat, protested that he had in fact tried to aid the princess. Rat, a trained paramedic, said that he attempted to take Diana's pulse before stepping back to snap pictures of the car after help arrived. After 48 hours of questioning, all seven were freed, but Romuald Rat and Christian Martinez, one of the other photographers in the group, were stripped of their press passes and forced to post bail. The police dragnet for suspects among the paparazzi widened until a total of 10 were under investigation by the end of September.

Although not yet officially charged with any crime, the paparazzi had already been convicted in the court of public opinion. Other witnesses on the scene shortly after the accident accused the photojournalists of everything from interfering with rescue personnel to snatching jewelry from Princess Diana's mortally injured body. Even tabloid readers suffered attacks of guilt. An anonymous E-mail message to Diana's memorial web page on the Internet addressed the princess. "I was selfish," it read. "I watched, I listened, I picked up the magazines that had your picture. . . . I was wrong. Please believe me, I never wanted you to suffer. . . . I did not understand, until I saw the news

*In the massive outpouring of grief over Diana's death, well-wishers carpeted the path to Kensington Palace with flowers, notes, stuffed animals, and other tokens of affection.*

about your death, how badly we treated you."

Just days after the tragedy, the furor surrounding the methods of tabloid journalism was refueled when color pictures of the princess, trapped and clearly visible through the crushed car's windows, were offered for one-quarter of a million dollars on the world market. Before it was even confirmed that such photos existed, American editor Stephen Coz publicly announced that his paper, the *National Enquirer*, would never consider buying them. Coz urged other publishers to follow suit, saying, "a line has to be drawn."

In the end, although a German newspaper ran one image showing one or two figures slumped in the car, no papers ran any photos clearly showing Diana or the other crash victims. But journalists still sought inside information about the princess's last moments. Rumors ran rampant about Diana's private "last words" for Prince Charles, her sons, and Dodi al-Fayed and his family.

One person who claimed that he could put those rumors to rest—as well as the talk of misconduct by the paparazzi—was a French physician named Frédéric Maillez, who was the first doctor to reach Diana. He had been driving in the opposite lane of the highway when he saw the crash. In an interview with the *Times* of London in late November 1997, Maillez said that the princess was in extreme pain when he reached her. "She kept saying how much she hurt as I gently put a resuscitation mask over her mouth," he recalled. As for any memorable "last words," however, Dr. Maillez was close-mouthed: "If there were other words from the princess," he said, "I cannot remember them and would not repeat them if I could." The French doctor also remembered being aware of the photographers, but he stoutly maintained that they had bothered no one. "I could not let these charges of bad behavior and interfering with the body stick—they simply weren't true," he said.

Debate over whether the paparazzi contributed to Diana's death rages on. Many people felt both anger and guilt over how hungrily the press stalked Diana throughout her public life and how eagerly they themselves had consumed her image. But some placed at least part of the responsibility squarely on Diana's shoulders. The princess, they maintained, had a love-hate relationship with the paparazzi. On April 1, 1997, for example, Diana had an angry exchange with a photographer who lurked outside her gym, and she asked a passerby to yank the film from the paparazzo's camera, which he did. On the evening of her death, however, Diana had told a friend, *Daily Mail* correspondent Richard Kay, about her imminent return to England. "I'm coming home tomorrow," she told him. "The boys will be back from Scotland in the evening. I will have a few days with them before they're back at school." Richard Kay would then presumably show up

*Pallbearers carry the body of Diana, Princess of Wales, out of the Paris hospital where she was pronounced dead only hours earlier.*

to turn Diana's reunion with Wills and Harry into an upbeat photo opportunity.

Reeling with shock and rage over Diana's death, people frantically sought someone to blame. After the photographers, the next candidate was obvious. Driver Henri Paul had received instruction at Germany's Mercedes antiterrorist driving school. But Paul's driving skills were not in question; his sobriety was. Reportedly, he was not scheduled to work on the night of the crash until Dodi al-Fayed hastily enlisted him to drive his getaway car while a chauffeur drove the decoy car. Just hours before receiving these orders, Henri Paul was spotted drinking whiskey and beer in a bar. Preliminary autopsy results found that his blood alcohol level was 1.75 grams per liter, more than three times the legal limit of 0.5 in France. (A subsequent test placed his blood alcohol at four times the limit.) Medical examiners also detected an antidepressant drug and a drug used to treat alcoholism in Paul's system.

In early 1998, the ongoing investigation into the crash revealed that Henri Paul was known to be an alcoholic by his fellow employees at the Ritz. The probe also revealed that, shortly before the fatal drive, he had told waiting photographers gathered outside the Ritz about Dodi and Diana's plans to leave. Paul's drinking, high-speed driving, and evident betrayal of Dodi al-Fayed appeared to exonerate the French photographers still living under official suspicion of manslaughter in the case. In 1998, police also continued looking into whether Henri Paul's vehicle sideswiped a white Fiat Uno before careening out of control, as some eyewitnesses contended.

In addition to riding with a drunk driver, Princess Diana had made a second fatal mistake: she was not wearing a seat belt at the time of the crash. In fact, Trevor Rees-Jones—the only survivor—was also the only one in the Mercedes to buckle up.

As anger gave way to sadness over this senseless

tragedy, the world joined Great Britain in its grief. On the Sunday morning following the crash, flowers, notes, and stuffed animals began to pile up in front of Kensington and Buckingham Palaces, creating mountains of loving tributes that would ultimately reach several feet in height. Volunteers later cleared them from the courtyards and donated the salvageable flowers and gifts to charity.

Diana had been dead only a few hours when Prince Charles accompanied her sisters, Lady Sarah McCorquodale and Lady Jane Fellowes, to Paris to claim the

*In a rare public show of affection, Prince Charles (right, wearing kilt) holds his son Harry's hand as they view tributes to Princess Diana outside Balmoral Castle on September 4, 1997. Prince Philip, Duke of Edinburgh (center) and Prince William (right) are seen in the background.*

princess's body. Charles reportedly spent 30 minutes paying his respects to Diana. The couple had recently seemed to reach a public truce; when together they watched Harry compete in Ludgrove School's sports day in June of that year, they had appeared relaxed and friendly. The prince brought Diana home in a casket draped in the maroon and gold flag of the British monarchy (though a member of the royal family, Diana did not have her own royal standard). After the plane touched down at Northolt's Royal Air Force base, Diana's coffin was borne on the shoulders of an honor guard dressed in gray uniforms.

The world watched. That evening, those who could crowd into London's St. Paul's Cathedral—where a fairy tale had begun with such promise 16 years earlier—attended a memorial service for Diana. The next day, Britons lined up more than a mile deep to sign five condolence books at St. James Palace. That afternoon 11 more books were added—and the line kept growing until the 43rd book filled with messages of love for the "People's Princess" was closed three weeks later.

Around the world, people flocked to sign other books of condolence housed in British embassies. American women in particular seemed to share England's sense of loss. Diana had, after all, reinvented herself as a living ideal of modern Western womanhood: a hard worker, a devoted mother, a fashion trendsetter—and a woman who could stand on her own. "I didn't realize how much I liked her," was a common refrain among those who remembered her.

Dignitaries and commoners alike weighed in with their feelings about Diana. Mother Teresa, the Nobel Peace Prize–winning nun from Calcutta whose works had inspired the princess, remembered Diana as "a very great friend, in love with the poor." (The 87-year-old Mother Teresa followed Diana in death just five days later, on September 5.) "We liked her very much. We admired her work," said President Bill Clinton. In

*The solemn funeral procession of Princess Diana makes its way to Westminster Abbey, September 6, 1997. Following the flag-draped casket are Prince Philip, Prince William, Earl Spencer, Prince Harry, and Prince Charles.*

London, the ordinary folk who gathered to lay flowers outside of Kensington Palace felt that the princess belonged to them in a way that no born royal ever could. One mourner, a 22-year-old engineer named Jamie Wood, said it best: "I think we have lost our queen today."

Stories of everyday kindnesses Diana had performed outside of the spotlight began to emerge. "She used to pop in at the middle of the night to see who else couldn't sleep at 2:00 A.M.," recalled Paul Theobold, a resident of London Lighthouse, an AIDS treatment facility. Eight-year-old Danielle Stephenson told of Diana's frequent visits and phone calls when the child was confined to the Royal Brompton Hospital for a rare heart condition. "We used to joke with her about whether she wore a crown or sat on a throne and she'd always laugh," the little girl remembered as she laid a bouquet of sunflowers outside of Kensington Palace.

Even less-than-ardent admirers shared the sense of Diana's special place among royalty. "I've never been a royal watcher, a royal lover," said London cab driver Tony Rubin. "But in my opinion, she was the only one worth anything out of the whole lot of 'em."

In the week following Diana's death, more Britons would adopt Rubin's opinion. People were outraged to learn that on the Sunday of the accident the royal family members, who were at Balmoral, took the newly motherless young princes to church as usual, then forbade mention of Diana's name during prayers for the dead. As her subjects wept openly outside Buckingham Palace, the queen remained at Balmoral. When the people wanted the Union Jack (the national flag of Great Britain) flown at half-mast over Buckingham Palace in Diana's honor, the Palace refused because the royal standard traditionally flies there, and only when the monarch is in residence.

The Windsors' inflexibility and unwillingness to return from Scotland in the aftermath of Diana's death caused a public backlash against them. Tabloid newspapers ran confrontational headlines: "Your people are suffering," the *Mirror* exhorted the queen. "Speak to us Ma'am."

Queen Elizabeth II soon reconsidered her original plans to return to London just in time for Diana's funeral, which was slated for Saturday, September 6. The queen and Prince Philip were back at Buckingham Palace before the week's end, which meant that the royal standard could now fly at half-mast. More important, the queen and her husband mingled with the crowd gathered at the palace gates, clasping their hands, talking with them, accepting bouquets and mementos in Diana's memory. Prince Charles followed suit, taking Princes William and Harry to see the tributes laid outside Kensington Palace. Their behavior was suddenly reminiscent of that of the People's Princess herself.

Queen Elizabeth II went still further to console her people. That Friday, she made a historic televised statement about the princess. "I admired her and respected her for her energy and her commitment to others, and especially for her devotion to her two boys," she said. "No one who knew Diana will ever forget her."

As the funeral drew near, a Buckingham Palace spokesman promised that it would be "very much a unique funeral for a unique person." Diana was no longer an official member of the royal family; she was therefore no longer entitled to a state funeral. At the same time, the House of Windsor knew that it was crucial to treat Diana in death with the respect that many accused them of withholding during her lifetime, so it was careful to respond to the people's wishes. For example, the Palace lengthened the route Diana's coffin would take to Westminster Abbey when the British Parliament pointed out that the original route would be choked off by the sheer number of people expected to line the streets. Television screens nearly 5 meters (16

*Diana's friend Elton John sang a moving version of his song "Candle in the Wind" during the princess's funeral service. John donated all proceeds from the song to charity.*

feet) high and nearly 7 meters (22 feet) wide were erected in Hyde Park for those who were not among the 1,900 guests invited to the abbey.

An estimated two million people turned out for the procession on Saturday morning, September 6, 1997; another two billion TV viewers watched the day's events. London was mild and sunny—and strewn with flowers. Diana's casket, still draped in the royal flag, made the $5\frac{1}{2}$-kilometer journey (about $3\frac{1}{2}$ miles) from Kensington Palace to Westminster Abbey atop a horse-drawn gun carriage surrounded by red-coated Welsh Guardsmen. The coffin was adorned with white lilies from the Spencer family, a bouquet of white tulips from Wills, and a small circle of white roses bearing a card that read "Mummy" in Prince Harry's boyish handwriting. Diana's younger brother, Charles, the ninth Earl Spencer, walked abreast of Princes Charles, Philip, William, and Harry as they solemnly trailed behind the carriage.

The boy princes, bravely maintaining their composure as they made the saddest walk of their young lives, were the object of special affection and concern. Queen Elizabeth II, however, amazed onlookers most of all. She stood on the roadside near Buckingham Palace to view the coffin. As it passed, the queen—a woman not obligated to bow to anyone on earth—did just that. It was an unprecedented show of respect for the former daughter-in-law who had prized intuition over protocol.

The royal family had requested that no pictures be taken of them inside cavernous Westminster Abbey. It scarcely mattered. All eyes were on the Spencer family as they said goodbye to their beloved sister and daughter. Lady Sarah McCorquodale, the sister Diana had worshiped as a little girl, read a short poem about love; Prime Minister Tony Blair read a biblical passage on the same topic. Few in the church were able to withhold tears when Diana's longtime friend Elton John sang a version of his ode to Marilyn Monroe, "Candle in the Wind," with lyrics rewritten especially for Diana:

Goodbye England's Rose;
> may you ever grow in our hearts.
You were the grace that placed itself
> where lives were torn apart.
You called out to our country,
> and you whispered to those in pain.
Now you belong to heaven,
> and the stars spell out your name. . . .

Earl Spencer's eulogy provided the funeral's most dramatic moments, though. In it, he remembered "the unique, complex, extraordinary, and irreplaceable Diana, whose beauty, both internal and external, will never be extinguished from our minds." At the same time, he reminded the congregation of her vulnerability—her childlike need to do good in order to feel worthy of love—and he suggested that they remember her not as a saint but as a remarkable and imperfect person.

Having commemorated his sister, Earl Spencer then challenged and chastised the royal establishment and the press. In a bold reference to the queen's decision to strip Diana of the honorific title "Her Royal Highness" after her divorce from Prince Charles, Earl Spencer noted that Diana "needed no royal title to continue to generate her particular brand of magic." He then turned the world's attention to his nephews. He vowed that he and the rest of William and Harry's "blood family" would make sure they grew up "so that their souls are not simply immersed by duty and tradition, but can sing openly as [Diana] planned." He did not spare the media a parting shot, either: playing off of the princess's namesake, the Roman goddess of the hunt,

Earl Spencer pointed out the irony of his sister's short life as "the most hunted person of the modern age."

The crowd outside the abbey cheered its approval of the ninth Earl Spencer's rousing speech. If Britain's collective heartache was not obvious by the ceremony's end, the trip to Diana's final resting place made it unmistakable. As the limousine bearing her casket wended its way 120 kilometers (75 miles) north of London to the village of Great Brington and the Spencers' Althorp estate, flowers tossed by mourners along the route threatened to cover the windshield entirely. Diana, Princess of Wales, was privately buried on a tiny island in the center of a lake on the grounds of Althorp. It seemed fitting: although she had dreaded moving to Althorp as a girl, the adult Diana had claimed to do her best soul-searching near water.

The greatest tragedy of Diana's death was that she seemed to have just begun to master her life when it was taken from her. The princess was truly a work in progress. Not only had she survived the utter destruction of her former life when she joined the House of Windsor, but she had also battled her own personal demons to become an exemplary parent and a source of comfort and strength for others. Once scorned by Prince Charles, Diana nevertheless proved that she had a mind and a life of her own.

Diana's slow but steady maturation into a global ambassador for the sick, the forgotten, and the weak had taken most people by surprise. No one could have predicted the scope and intensity of the emotion surrounding her death. A blur of Diana-related events and news items continued unabated even after her burial. The royal family immediately established the Diana, Princess of Wales, Memorial Fund to benefit the causes she championed. Within days, contributions began pouring in. Elton John donated all proceeds from sales of his tribute song, "Candle in the Wind '97," enriching the fund to approximately $60 million by the end of the year. In January 1998, Earl Spencer unveiled plans to open his sister's gravesite to the public from July 1 to August 31. Ticketholders would pay about $15 to see Diana's burial plot, with all proceeds going to her memorial fund.

Not all of the events following her death were positive, however. Critics of Earl Spencer's plan accused him of turning Diana's grave into a British version of Graceland, the former home of American rock-and-roll idol Elvis Presley. Even before his announcement, though, was the bombshell revelation that Diana herself was Andrew Morton's source for *Diana: Her True Story*. Morton and Diana had kept their collaboration a well-guarded secret. "If she assisted me, what's in it for her?" he had protested when the tell-all biography first came out in 1992. "Her friends, her family, her counselors, even her astrologer all helped me. But not the Princess of Wales." Less than a month after Diana's untimely death, however, Andrew Morton unveiled a new edition, *Diana: Her True Story—In Her Own Words*. In addition to a new foreword and an additional chapter covering Diana's death, the revised book included an 18,000-word transcript compiled from six secret interviews with the princess. The royal family's suspicion that Diana had aided Morton directly was finally confirmed. Although *Diana: Her True Story—In Her Own Words* was an immediate best-seller, Dodi al-Fayed's father, Mohamed, refused to sell it in Harrods department store.

Al-Fayed may not have allowed the book in his store, but he later drew criticism for selling cheap dolls in Diana's likeness. The problem of merchants cashing in on Diana's death grew until former prime minister John Major said he planned to take the matter to court so that any profits from unlicensed Diana products would go to Princes William and Harry.

As 1997 drew to a close, it was clear that Diana's myth showed no signs of dying with her. British econ-

*Tributes to Diana line the steps of the British embassy in Washington, D.C. "She was the People's Princess and that is how she will stay," British Prime Minister Tony Blair said of her.*

omists attributed sluggish sales of consumer goods in September and October to the "Diana effect." They theorized that people's grief had dampened their interest in shopping. At the same time, psychiatrists noted that in the months following Diana's funeral, admissions to mental hospitals had dropped drastically. The cleansing effect of a good cry over the dead princess was credited with improving the nation's collective mental health.

Some doubted the power of Diana's ghost, however. In the week-long spasm of grief that gripped London after the fatal crash, a few were still quick to point out that Diana would have lived a privileged but uneventful life had she not married into the monarchy. Others cited her less-than-saintly side: "None of them [the media] dares mention her mercurial mood swings, and you

don't see interviews with the many members of her personal staff who quit on her," mused one retired school-
master in response to the flood of tears and tributes.

"It is clear that there are two Dianas," surmised
Andrew Morton, "the individual known to her friends
and family, and now the venerated icon, the projection
of millions of fantasies, hopes, and dreams." Diana,
Princess of Wales, crowded more living into 36 years
than many of us ever will. She could indeed be moody,
naive, and at times even manipulative. But far more
often she was warm, humorous, energetic, and gifted
with the ability to give those hovering on the margins
of society a sense of their own importance and value.
All it took was her smile, her touch, and her uncanny
ability to listen.

Perhaps Queen Elizabeth II and Prince Philip took
their cue from the best of Diana's character on November 20, 1997, the day of their 50th wedding anniversary.
The royal couple sold a limited number of tickets to
their celebration at Windsor Castle to anyone who
wished to attend. It was seen as an unprecedented move
toward warmth and accessibility by the monarchy.

Time will tell whether Diana's "common touch" will
live on in Princes William and Harry, but the tragic story
of the princess who died a heroine for the world's lonely
and powerless will last forever. "I knew my life was going
to be a winding road," she told biographer Andrew Morton during one of their clandestine interviews.

How right she was.

## THE DIANA, PRINCESS OF WALES, MEMORIAL FUND:

Kensington Palace
London W8 4PU United Kingdom

*OR:*

P.O. Box 1
London WC1B 5HW United Kingdom

# CHRONOLOGY

1961  Born the Honorable Diana Spencer on July 1, the third surviving child of Viscount Althorp (Edward John "Johnnie" Spencer) and Frances Ruth Burke Roche Spencer

1967  Johnnie and Frances separate

1969  The Spencers' divorce becomes final; Johnnie wins custody of their four children

1977  Meets Charles, Prince of Wales, through her sister Sarah

1981  Becomes engaged to Prince Charles on February 24; married on July 29

1982  Prince William Arthur Philip Louis ("Wills") born June 21

1984  Prince Henry Charles Albert David ("Harry") born September 15

1986  Rumors begin circulating about Diana's bulimia; breakdown of the Waleses' marriage is noticed by the public

1992  Andrew Morton's book, *Diana: Her True Story*, published in June, reveals her jealousy over Charles's affair and her five suicide attempts; on August 25 the *Sun* publishes excerpts of Diana's phone conversation with James Gilbey; on December 9 Prime Minister John Major announces Diana and Charles's separation

1993  Delivers "time and space speech" announcing her retirement from public life on December 3

1994  Prince Charles gives televised interview on June 29, in which he admits to adultery; book *Princess in Love*, allegedly chronicling Diana's five-year affair with riding instructor James Hewitt, released in late summer

1995  Gives first solo interview for BBC-TV's *Panorama*, admitting to an affair with Hewitt, claiming the royal family blocked her public work, and saying she does not wish to divorce Charles

1996  Agrees to begin divorce proceedings on July 12; divorce becomes final on August 28

1997  Visits land-mine victims in Angola in January; donates her gowns for a charity auction in New York that nets over $3.2 million; visits Bosnia to work toward eliminating land mines; dies in Paris automobile accident with companion Dodi al-Fayed on August 31; buried September 6 at Althorp estate

Campbell, Lady Colin. *Diana in Private*. New York: St. Martin's Press, 1992.

Clarke, Mary. *Little Girl Lost*. New York: Carol Publishing Group, 1996.

Diana, Princess of Wales. 1995. Interview by Martin Bashir. *Panorama*. BBC-TV, 20 November.

Green, Michelle. "Inside the Palace." *People* (Special Collector's Issue), Fall 1997.

Holden, Anthony. *The Tarnished Crown*. New York: Random House, Inc., 1993.

Horyn, Cathy. "Diana Reborn." *Vanity Fair*, July 1997.

Junor, Penny. *Diana: Princess of Wales*. Garden City, NY: Doubleday & Company, 1983.

Kantrowitz, Barbara. "Collapse of a Marriage." *Newsweek* (Commemorative Issue), Fall 1997.

Monckton, Rosa. "My Friend Diana." *Newsweek* (Commemorative Issue), Fall 1997.

Morton, Andrew. *Diana: Her New Life*. New York: Simon & Schuster, 1994.

_____. *Diana: Her True Story—In Her Own Words* (revised edition). New York: Simon & Schuster, 1997.

Mulligan, Hugh A. "An Undercurrent in London." *Philadelphia Inquirer*, 5 September 1997.

# INDEX

# INDEX

# PICTURE CREDITS

2: AP/Wide World Photos
8: AP/Wide World Photos
10: AP/Wide World Photos
13: AP/Wide World Photos
14: AP/Wide World Photos
18: UPI/Corbis-Bettmann
21: AP/Wide World Photos
22: AP/Wide World Photos
25: AP/Wide World Photos
26: AP/Wide World Photos
30: AP/Wide World Photos
32: AP/Wide World Photos
37: AP/Wide World Photos
38: AP/Wide World Photos
40: AP/Wide World Photos
43: UPI/Corbis-Bettmann
46: UPI/Corbis-Bettmann
49: AP/Wide World Photos
50: AP/Wide World Photos
54: AP/Wide World Photos

57: AP/Wide World Photos
58: UPI/Corbis-Bettmann
62: UPI/Corbis-Bettmann
64: AP/Wide World Photos
66: AP/Wide World Photos
70: AP/Wide World Photos
73: AP/Wide World Photos
74: AP/Wide World Photos
76: AP/Wide World Photos
78: AP/Wide World Photos
81: Reuters/Corbis-Bettmann
83: AP/Wide World Photos
85: Reuters/Corbis-Bettmann
86: AP/Wide World Photos
90: AP/Wide World Photos
93: AP/Wide World Photos
96: AP/Wide World Photos
98: AP/Wide World Photos

103: AP/Wide World Photos
104: AP/Wide World Photos
107: AP/Wide World Photos
109: AP/Wide World Photos
111: AP/Wide World Photos
114: Reuters/Corbis-Bettmann
116: AP/Wide World Photos
117: Reuters/Corbis-Bettmann
119: AP/Wide World Photos
121: AP/Wide World Photos
123: AP/Wide World Photos
125: AP/Wide World Photos
128: AP/Wide World Photos
132: Agence France Presse/Corbis-Bettmann
134: AP/Wide World Photos

**Kristine Brennan** is a writer and editor in the Philadelphia area, where she lives with her husband and son. She holds a B.A. in English with a concentration in Professional Writing from Elizabethtown College. This is her first book for Chelsea House.